God

WILL NOT FAIL YOU

Other Books by Samuel Doctorian

The Life Story of Samuel Doctorian Begins at Calvary
My Daily Strength, A Daily Devotional
Heavenly Beings, Angels–Are They Real?

Also by Jasmine Doctorian Workman

God's Word: My Precious Legacy

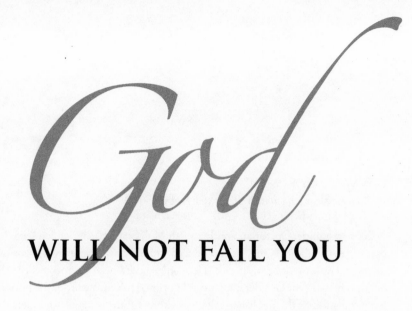

God
WILL NOT FAIL YOU

A LIFE OF MIRACLES
IN THE MIDDLE EAST AND BEYOND

Rev. Samuel Doctorian
with Elizabeth Moll Stalcup, Ph.D.

BELIEVE BOOKS
Life Stories That Inspire
WASHINGTON, DC

GOD WILL NOT FAIL YOU
By Samuel Doctorian with Elizabeth Moll Stalcup, Ph.D.

Unless otherwise noted, all Scripture quotations are from the *Holy Bible, King James Version* (KJV).

Other Scripture quotations taken from the *Holy Bible, New King James Version* (NKJV). © 1982 by Thomas Nelson, Inc. Used by permission. All rights reserved.

ISBN: 0-9787428-5-0
Library of Congress Control Number: 2006933287

Cover design: *Jack Kotowicz, Washington, D.C., VelocityDesignGroup.com*
Layout design: *Annie Kotowicz and Jen Anderson*

Believe Books publishes the inspirational life stories of extraordinary believers in God from around the world. Requests for information should be addressed to **Believe Books** at www.believebooks.com. **Believe Books** is a registered trade name of **Believe Books, LLC** of Washington, D.C.

Printed in the United States of America

To my wife, Naomi, and our five children, Paul, Jasmine, Daniel, Samuel, Jr., and Luther John. May the Lord use this book for His Glory and to build His kingdom!
—Samuel

To my husband, Sam—what a blessing you are to me!
—Elizabeth

CONTENTS

Preface ix

Acknowledgments xii

Foreword...xiii

1   Tsunami!...1

2   Armenia, My Armenia 3

3   Jerusalem 11

4   Give Us This Day Our Daily Bread 15

5   Leaving School 19

6   Bible School..25

7   Where is the Money?...29

8   Baptized in the Holy Ghost.......................................33

9   To Scotland..39

10 Providential Lunch..43

11 Preaching in Great Britain 47

12 Revival and Ordination..51

13 Call to the Middle East 55

14 Back in the Middle East 59

15 Marrying Naomi 63

16 Call to Egypt..67

17 Revival in Damascus..73

18 The Death of a Boy and the Conversion of a Spiritualist 79

19 Revival in Egypt..87

20 On Fire in Egypt...93

21 Secret Police...101

22 The Woman on Death Row.......................................105

23 America 109

24 Beirut..117

25 Bible School and Christian Day School 123

26 Brazil and Beyond 127

27 To the Nations...131

28 Traveling the Bible Lands and the World........................135

29 Revival in Portugal 151

30 Miracle Water!..157

31 Revival in London...161

32 War in Lebanon 165

33 Fire Worshipper 169

34 Bombs, Cars, and Bibles 175

35 Voyage on a Cattle Ship 183

36 Blacklisted!..189

37 Bible Land Tours...197

38 Healing Touch...199

39 Ireland 203

40 My Healing...207

41 Swiss Psychiatrist..211

42 My Manager, the Holy Spirit.......................................215

43 Tiny Countries, Big Hearts 221

44 My Family..227

45 Indonesia...231

46 Resurrection!..235

47 Baptism in the River Jordan..239

48 On Patmos 245

49 On Television in the Middle East 251

Epilogue 255

PREFACE

For more than 50 years I have been traveling around the world preaching the Word of God. Even though I am old and tired, I travel all but a few weeks of the year to Africa, Indonesia, Singapore, South America, Europe and the Middle East. I often feel weary, but when I get up to preach, I am filled with the mighty Holy Ghost and the fatigue lifts. I love to see sinners turn to God and cry out to Him, for He alone can save.

I preach all over the world, sharing the miracles, wonders, and supernatural acts of God in my life. Ephesians 3:20 says that God ". . . is able to do exceedingly abundantly above all that we ask or think, according to the power that worketh in us." The Lord has performed tremendous miracles in my life. People often say, "Why don't you write a book about these great acts of God?"

Up until now, I have never wanted anybody to write my life story. Other people have asked if they could write it, but I did not say "yes" to them. Now I have been praying daily, and I am fully persuaded that this dear chosen vessel, Elizabeth, should write it now. It is the right time to share the great wonders that the Lord has done.

I pray that you will be blessed by reading how God has blessed this unworthy life so abundantly. I pray these stories will increase your faith, and I hope and pray that you will give the glory to God for all He has done.

Samuel Doctorian
Pasadena, California

I had just fallen asleep when my son came home. "Mom, there was an amazing speaker at youth group tonight. I think you are supposed to write a book about him."

I blinked my eyes and stared at the business card Sammy was holding out to me. The tiny picture on the card showed a man with a long snow-white beard and a wide grin. *He looks like Santa Claus*, I thought. "Okay, Sammy," I said, closing my eyes.

"You have to call him tomorrow," my son urged. "He is leaving for Singapore in two days."

"Okay," I promised, as I rolled over.

In the morning I studied the card, which read *Bible Land Mission*. People who know I am a writer are always telling me that I should write a book about this or that person but nothing ever comes of it. But a promise is a promise, so I picked up the phone and dialed the number on the card.

A man with a charming accent answered the phone. We spoke for a few minutes. "So you want to write my life story," he said. *Do I?* I wondered. I wasn't sure. I didn't know anything about his life, but I didn't want to tell him what I was thinking, so I said nothing. Sammy was at school so I couldn't quiz him. All I learned during that short phone call was that Samuel Doctorian was a friend of some dear friends of ours and that he was staying at their place.

It was hard to imagine how it would all come together. But many times over the next year, as I would seek God, He would whisper to my heart. "Do not be afraid to write this book."

This has been a journey of faith for all of us—Samuel, my family and I, and Believe Books, the publishing company—as we have watched God bring everything together. He has given us the courage and strength to persevere. It has been hard for Samuel to take time from his exhausting schedule to answer my many questions about the details of his life. Our publisher, Believe Books has heard God's call to publish inspirational life stories and has moved ahead in faith, trusting God to stretch their resources to launch this venture. And I have learned to trust God to inspire the writing of this book and to provide for all my needs along the way.

This is the first fruit of our labors together, and we hope that this book will be the first of many. We believe that we are called. We believe God has a blessing for you, dear reader, in this book. We have overcome. God has not failed us!

To God be the glory!
Elizabeth Moll Stalcup
Reston, Virginia

ACKNOWLEDGMENTS

The authors would like to thank George and Gretchen Keitt for marking up an early version of the manuscript with many helpful corrections. We also thank Naomi Doctorian for carefully going over every story and making sure every detail was completely accurate. Two are better than one, especially when it comes to remembering a shared history. Kathy Moll and Marilyn Henretty caught many errors we had missed and Shirley "Eagle-eye" Howson armed with her *Chicago Manual of Style*, combed through the book catching inconsistencies, to which we were completely blind.

Paul and Danny Doctorian culled through family pictures and sent them to us to be included in the book.

Elizabeth also thanks her family, troopers par excellence, for a phenomenal amount of support in the form of running errands, cooking meals, and doing housework while she was glued to the computer. There were days she would not have eaten, if not for them.

Without all of you and the sustaining strength of Almighty God, we could not have written this book!

FOREWORD

It is a great privilege to be invited to write the foreword to Samuel Doctorian's latest book. I have known Brother Samuel for over 30 years and have traveled with him to 27 different countries. During that time I am always amazed at the messages that the Lord gives him.

Samuel's messages are powerful, evangelistic, anchored in solid exegesis with sound homiletics. They are biblical, but not preachy; contemporary but not trendy. He gives illustrations that bring conviction to your heart.

Samuel's Christianity shines through every part of his life. He lives in a way that goes beyond expectation and explanation. His actions speak louder than even the most carefully chosen words.

He preaches Spirit-filled messages—with no ranting or screaming—in an earnest, tender tone proclaiming the Gospel in an arousing, surprising and often alarming way.

This book will touch your hearts and bring you closer to the Lord as you read it and find His richest and choicest blessings.

Pastor George McRobb
Boddam United Free Church of Scotland
Aberdeen, Scotland

1

Tsunami!

It was the worst nightmare! But it was not a nightmare, it was a vision from God. I sat up in bed, trembling, as tears ran down my cheeks. God had just shown me a vision of a gigantic earthquake and the land covered by water. Flooding. Thousands drowning. Destruction everywhere. I was overwhelmed by grief.

"Lord," I cried. "What is this? Do you want me to leave Indonesia right now?"

"No," the Lord said. "Finish your meetings first."

I was staying in the five-star Sheraton Hotel in Surabaya, Indonesia. It was early Sunday morning, December 19, 2004. In just a few hours I was supposed to preach at the 6:00 A.M. service. Indonesia is so hot that the 6:00 A.M. service draws 8,000 people. Following that I was to preach at two smaller services, at 8:00 A.M. and 3:30 P.M.

That day, I preached as scheduled. The next day I officiated at the wedding of two dear friends. Then I flew to Singapore where I stayed for four days preaching, praying for the sick and teaching. On December 25, I flew home to California. Even before the plane landed, a magnitude 9.0 earthquake had ripped the ocean floor off the eastern end of Sumatra, creating a wave that flooded the entire region claiming over 186,000 lives. This was unmistakably the tsunami I had seen in my vision just six days before.

2

Armenia, My Armenia

I was born in 1930, in Beirut, the capital of Lebanon, into an Armenian family. When I was a small child, I had very few aunts and uncles and no grandparents because the Turks had slaughtered all our loved ones during the Armenian Genocide. Everyone knows how the Nazis tried to eliminate the Jews during World War II, but very few people know that during World War I, the Ottoman Turks tried to annihilate the Armenian people. Many were massacred because they would not deny Christ. Others were forced from their homes and driven hundreds of miles on foot, out into the Syrian desert where they died of hunger and thirst under the scorching sun.

It was a terrible time. The Turks abused our women and children, and took all of our possessions—farms, homes and valuables. They tried to wipe the Armenian people from the face of the earth. Nearly two million—two-thirds—of the Armenian people perished and thousands more were driven from their land.

Before the massacre began, my grandparents had lived peacefully with the Turks, side by side in the village of Severag, near the town of Ourfa, just 30 miles north of the Syrian border. The area where my grandparents lived had once been part of Armenia, but at this point in history, the Young Turks who ruled the Ottoman Empire had seized the entire region making that area also part of Turkey.

My grandfather was a famous surgeon—indeed Doctorian means *family of a doctor* in Armenian. He treated both Armenians and Turks, but his years of service to them did not save him. The Turks came for him one day and shot him as he tried to flee on his horse. My loved ones counted 25 bullets in his body as they laid him in his grave.

A few days later, the Turks came for the women and children. My grandmother and her six sons were taken down to the banks of the Euphrates River where the Turks demanded that they deny Christ, or have their heads chopped off with an axe.

One of the Turkish soldiers pulled my father, who was only nine years old, out of the line and hid him in a cave. My father did not want to leave his mother. He did not realize that this soldier was saving his life. He begged to stay with his mother and brothers. But the soldier told him, "No. Be quiet. Stay here."

When the Turks demanded that my dear grandmother deny Christ, she refused, saying, "I will not." She laid her head down on the chopping block and the Turks ended her life with an axe, and threw her headless body into the river. So many were slaughtered during that dreadful time, that for weeks, the mighty Euphrates River ran red with blood.

Everyone who would not deny Christ perished. My 17-year-old auntie, like all the young women, was pulled out of the line by the soldiers and tortured in unimaginable ways. After they abused my dear auntie, they cut off her hands and threw her into a well to drown. Of the entire family, only my father survived.

After the slaughter, the soldier came back to the cave where my father sat crying. The soldier had saved my father's life, sparing him because my grandfather had once saved his life. But it was an evil time. The soldier saved my father from the axe, only to sell him in the market. My father was just a young boy, but he became a slave in a Muslim home. They changed his name to *Abdallah*, which means "slave of Allah." He remembered that his real name was *Boghos*, which is Armenian for "Paul."

For three years he served his Muslim masters, fetching water from the well, taking care of his master's children, and driving the camels to pasture. Many times he was beaten, hungry and cold, with only a hard crust of bread to eat. He grieved for his family and longed to escape.

He remembered how his mother would pray to someone named Jesus, so he used to pray, "Jesus of my mother, please help me." One day, he could stand it no longer. After herding the camels into the hills, he ran away. He had no idea where he was going. He ran through hills, frightened by the sight of human bones still lying on the ground, exposed to the elements. Many had starved on the forced march to Syria and thousands more had been killed because they could not keep up. Young women and girls were killed because they fought the soldiers who pulled them out of the lines to molest them. Thousands of bodies had been thrown into the rivers, and washed ashore where they lay exposed to the sun and rain. The Turks would not let anyone bury those that washed ashore. So for many years, in that part of Turkey, you could see the bones of dead saints lying on the ground, or bits of limbs poking from shallow graves.

For three days my father endured cold, hunger, and thirst. Then he could run no longer. Shivering and tormented by fears, he lay down on a rock to die. He wanted to cry, but he had no more tears. As he lay there, one last time he lifted his head toward heaven and prayed, "Jesus of my mother, please help me."

He needed water, bread and shelter. He needed someone to love him. He needed to know God, the Supreme Being, Who alone could deliver him from his wretched state.

While he was crying out to God, he saw three men walk toward him. *I must flee*, he thought, but had no more strength to run. He sank back onto the rock, thinking, *If they are my enemies, let them kill me. I am ready to die.* As they drew near, he looked up into their faces and saw . . . kindness. For the first time in three years, someone was smiling at him.

First, they gave him water to drink. Then they gave him food. They were American Mennonite missionaries who had come to Turkey and Syria after World War I to rescue those who had survived the Genocide. My father could not understand their language, but he knew he was safe because their eyes filled with tears as they looked on his pitiful condition. He tried to walk, but he was too weak. Gently they lifted him up and carried him to an orphanage.

* * *

In 1957, when I was 27 years old, I was invited to preach at a Mennonite convention in the state of Oregon. I was thanking the Mennonites for sending missionaries to feed the Armenians when they were dispossessed refugees starving after the Genocide. I was telling them my father's story when a very old man stood and began waving his hand. I stopped preaching and looked at him. Tears were flowing down his cheeks. He clearly wanted to say something, but he was too overcome with emotion to get it out. They passed him the microphone. "Brothers and sisters," he began haltingly, "remember the story I've told you, many times before, of how we found a boy beaten and near death? And how we gave him water to drink and bread to eat and carried him to an orphanage? That boy's name was *Boghos* 'Paul'."

I raced off the platform straight into the arms of that brother, who, many years before, had saved my father's life. We were hugging each other, weeping and praising God. The entire crowd— more than two thousand people—were weeping with us. The other two men had gone to glory, but this 84-year-old brother was still alive. What joy we had! I was filled with joy because I had found one of the missionaries who had saved my father's life, and he was so happy because the boy he had saved lived to have a son who was now preaching the Good News all over the world.

A few years later, when I was in my thirties, I met a woman named Marie Sarrafian Baker who was from this same part of Turkey. She had survived the Armenian Genocide because she had been away at school in Constantinople when the Turks came for her family. After the Genocide, she traveled all over the region searching for some trace of her loved ones. As she searched, she heard many peoples' stories and wrote a book that I later published called *My Beloved Armenia*.

In the book, she described how Armenian children were snatched from their parents and sold in the market place. She wrote of how the Turks herded thousands of Armenians into the desert where they died of hunger and thirst. She found thousands of bodies of young women packed into wells where they drowned, just like my dear auntie.

No one in Marie's family survived. All perished. After she gave up searching, she dedicated herself to working with young Armenian girls, some as young as 10, who had been rescued from Muslim harems after this terrible time.

So few people know about the suffering of the Armenian people, and even today there are entire websites that deny the Genocide ever occurred. But we Armenians know it is true. We have heard our own fathers and mothers tell of how our people suffered and went to their death with the name of Christ on their lips.

* * *

After my father was rescued by the Mennonites, he lived in an orphanage in Lebanon for several years, then for a brief time the missionaries took the children to Aleppo, just south of Turkey along the coast in Syria. In that orphanage-church in Aleppo, my father heard the Gospel of Jesus clearly for the first time. He gave his heart to the Lord and was wonderfully saved and filled with the power of the Holy Spirit.

While he was in Aleppo, something amazing happened. He was walking in the street with a group of Armenian boys when he heard a voice that sounded familiar. He turned. A boy was looking at him.

"Are you Boghos?" the boy asked.

My father nodded his head. "Are you Hanna?" *Hanna* is Armenian for "John."

It was his oldest brother, John! All these years, my father had thought he was dead, but somehow John had survived. They fell on each other, hugging and kissing, so thankful to be reunited after seven years apart. They had lost everything—parents, brothers, sister, grandparents, home and possessions, but God had brought them together on the streets of Aleppo. I do not know how John escaped the slaughter that day on the banks of the Euphrates, but somehow he had survived. At the time that they met, my uncle John was living in Aleppo, and working for the French Military, who, at that time, controlled Syria.

Later, the missionaries took my father and the other children back to Beirut, and it was there that my father met the little girl who would become his wife and my mother. She was also an orphan who had been sold into slavery. The Turks had killed her mother in front of her own eyes when she was six years old and until her death in May at the age of 96, she still remembered it. I used to pray, "Lord, let her forget her painful memories," but she did not forget. She remembered how the Turks murdered her mother, and snatched her six-month-old brother from his bed. She screamed, "That's my brother!" But they ignored her cries and she went to the grave without knowing what became of her baby brother.

My mother was then sold into slavery in a Turkish home, but her Uncle Vartan, a fighter with the Armenian resistance, rescued her. He found out where she was being held, and came by night on his horse, climbed in the window, clapped his hand over her mouth so she would not scream, and whispered into her ear, "It is Uncle Vartan." Then they galloped away on his horse.

Her uncle brought her to the same orphanage where my father was living. And so it was that my mother and father met, and eventually fell in love. The pastor of the orphanage, a pastor in the Armenian Evangelical Church, performed their marriage ceremony. A young man named Samuel Pashgian, who had also grown up in the orphanage—the man for whom I was later named—was the best man, and his wife, Marie, was the matron of honor.

3

Jerusalem

My parents were very poor because both were orphans without a family to help them get started in life. They had no possessions or land, so when I was young, we lived in a large Armenian refugee camp in Beirut. There thousands of Armenians lived in wooden huts packed close together. All had lost homes during the Genocide, and even after World War II ended, and the Turks were defeated, there was no advocate to make them give us back our homes.

One day, when I was just an infant, too young to remember, the whole refugee camp caught fire. I was in the house asleep and nearly perished in that fire. My father ran into the burning house and raced out with me in his arms. Within 10 minutes the whole house had turned to ashes. Later, we learned that arsonists who started the fire wanted that piece of land too, but they couldn't put the Armenian refugees out, so they burned the place to the ground! Today, the electric company of Beirut has a big building on the site where that refugee camp once stood.

After the fire, my father first moved our family to Tyre, on the southern coast of Lebanon, where he worked as a tailor. Then he moved us to Jerusalem because he had heard that the Nazarenes had opened a Christian school in Jerusalem, and he wanted his children to go there. By then there were four of us: my older brother was 10, I was eight, and my two younger brothers were six and four.

I still remember the trip to Jerusalem. My father had gone on ahead, and the rest of the family was riding in a car with my mother. We stopped at the border between Lebanon and Palestine, and a British soldier in his white and blue uniform opened the door of the car. (Back then, the British ruled Palestine.) The soldier peered inside at the four of us boys sitting side-by-side in the back seat. He looked at my young mother and said, in astonishment, "Are *all* these your boys?" My mother smiled and said a bit wearily, "Yes, they're my boys." Then he closed the door and we crossed into Palestine.

In Jerusalem, we lived in the Hinnom Valley, in the poorest part of Jerusalem where, in Old Testament times, they used to dump ashes from the sacrifices. In that place, my father became a leader in the Armenian Nazarene Church, serving first as an elder, and then as treasurer. He loved our pastor, Rev. Samuel Krikorian, very much and spent many evenings visiting members of the congregation with him.

Our home in Jerusalem had only one room. We four boys shared a mattress with a single blanket. We lined up in bed in the order of our birth: George, then me, Phillip and David. I was glad to be in the middle. When George pulled on the blanket, David got cold. When David pulled, George would shiver, but I was always toasty warm in the middle.

When I was nine years old our family went to Calvary. There is some disagreement among historians as to the exact site of our Lord's crucifixion, but like many, I am convinced that Jesus died on a rugged embankment, outside the city wall, just above a place called "The Garden Tomb." It is a bare and rocky hill with caves on the side that make the hillside look like a skull from a distance. Green cedars grow up the sides of the hill, and there are a few scattered olive trees on top. Today there is a Muslim cemetery on the top of the hill, and at the base, a small garden and sadly, a bus station.

But back when I was nine, there was no bus station and as I stood in that garden, near a large tree, looking at the rocky hill, I had a powerful vision of Christ, the Son of God. He was nailed to the cross, in great torment. I saw blood running from His hands, His feet and His side. I saw blood flowing from His head where it was pierced by the crown of thorns and from His back where He had been whipped in Pilate's hall. I saw the torture and the suffering and my eyes were filled with tears.

I fell to my knees and cried out to God, "Why did all this happen?" It seemed as if I could see the Lord's lips moving, saying to me. "Samuel, because I loved you. Because I loved you." My heart was broken when I heard those words. I knew then that Jesus had loved me with a pure love, an eternal love, a deep and strong love, a sacrificial love. I said, "Lord, if You loved me so much and have given Yourself for me, then I am going to love You and live for You from this day forward."

That day the Lord did something in my heart. This change was not imaginary. It was not just a change in my mind or a change in my feelings; it was a change in my heart. I received new birth. Old things passed away; truly, all things became new.

I stood up. Everything was changed. Nature was different. I was different. My loved ones were different. Everything seemed different because the heart of this little nine year old had changed.

No one can really know about this new birth until they have experienced it. I am glad that the Lord opened my eyes. I was dead in trespasses and sins, but He quickened me by His Spirit. I was condemned, but Jesus justified me. I was in the depths of sin, but He lifted me. I was far from God, but He brought me very close to His heart. I was lost, without hope, but now I had a glorious hope with Christ Jesus in my heart.

I wanted to tell everybody at school and everyone I met about the Lord and what He had done for me—and what He could do for them.

What a glorious experience! I am glad that the Spirit bears witness with my spirit today that I am a child of God. I was justified by faith. I was a child of the devil and instantly I became a child of God. What a miracle!

When I was nine, all I knew was that I was a sinner and that Jesus loved me and came to save me from my sins. The only thing I needed to do was pray humbly, "Lord, save me!" By simple trust He did save me. He can do the same for you. Hallelujah!

4

Give Us This Day Our Daily Bread

My family was so poor that my parents often struggled just to put bread on the table and to keep us in school. For many years, the only job my father could find was in a British military camp called Sarafand, many miles from home, where he worked as a tailor. The camp was near the seashore, north of Tel Aviv, a long journey from Jerusalem. Father would come home once a month bringing four Palestinian pounds, equal to about four British pounds. He would give some to the grocer, some to the baker, and some here and there, paying our bills, and then he would travel back to Sarafand. For years, our family saw him only once a month.

One day when I was about 10 years old, I came home from school, and asked my mother for a piece of bread. All four of us boys were hungry as usual and we all wanted bread, but my mother told us to go out and play. We raced out, but around 7 o'clock we came home hungrier than ever. "Mother, we are hungry," we clamored, but Mother would not speak to us. She only looked sad. She washed our hands, feet, and faces and told us, "Come children, come, and go to bed now. Pray your prayers and go to sleep."

"Mother," we said, "What is the matter with you? We are hungry. We want bread!" But Mother was silent. She made us kneel and pray and then said, "Goodnight, children." Then she turned down the gaslight and went to bed.

The four of us began to cry, each looking at the others completely bewildered, with tears rolling down our cheeks. We were hungry and Mother had put us to bed! Why was she being so cruel? What had we done that she would not feed us? Finally, we cried ourselves to sleep.

At two o'clock in the morning, I awoke crying. "Mother," I called.

She came close to me and whispered, "What do you want, Samuel?"

"Mother," I answered, "I cannot sleep. I want bread!"

She went and got me a cup of water. "Drink this," she said, handing it to me.

"Mother," I said, "I am not thirsty, I am hungry. I want bread." Even though the gaslight was low, I could see bright tears streaming down her face. When I saw her tears, I stopped crying, drank the water and went back to sleep.

When morning dawned, we woke up famished, with tears still in our eyes.

My mother was crying, too. She said, "Children, pray. We do not have any bread and I do not know what to do. I don't know when your father will come home next, and we have nothing to eat."

My mother did not dare tell anyone that we were hungry. She believed that we should tell only God.

We could not even think of going to school when we were so hungry, so we sat around the table, crying out to God, "Father send us bread. Father send us bread."

Meanwhile, unbeknownst to us, God was working a miracle. There was a sudden knock on the door. "Keep quiet, children," my mother urged. "Do not make any noise. Do not let anyone know that we are praying for bread. Only tell God about our need."

She wiped the tears from her eyes and went to the door. When she opened the door a man stepped inside bearing a basket full of bread and cheese.

"Here children," he said, "take this bread. Your Father sent it to you." I ran to the basket and tore off a big hunk of bread and stuffed it into my mouth, as only a hungry child can. I was so glad that my father had sent us bread.

Years later I learned that my earthly father had nothing to do with that basket of food! I went to the man who had brought us the bread that day and asked him, "Sarkis, what made you come to our house that morning, and give us that basket of food?"

"Samuel," he confided, "I bought that bread and cheese to take to my own family in Bethlehem. I had purchased my bus ticket, and was sitting on the bus, waiting for it to leave, when a voice within me said, 'Rise. Take your basket of food to the family down in the Valley of Hinnom.'

"At first I argued with God. I said, 'No, Lord, I am already late! I must get home quickly and get back to my business.' But the voice kept saying, 'Rise, take it to that family.' I protested, 'They do not need this bread.' But the voice within me kept saying, 'Rise and go. They need this bread.'"

"I could not disobey that voice," he continued. "The driver was getting ready to start the bus, so I yelled, 'Just a minute, just a minute,' and ran down the aisle. I told the driver to let me off. He reminded me that my ticket would be useless, but I only nodded my head and climbed off. I walked down into the Valley of Hinnom, to your house, an eight-minute walk from the station. I felt rather foolish, so before I knocked on the door, I paused and put my ear to the door. I could hear hungry children crying, 'Father, send us bread!' The moment I heard you children wailing, I could wait no longer. I knocked on the door and when your mother opened the door, I told all of you, 'Your Father sent this bread. Take it.' I gave the entire basket—everything I had bought—to you."

How wonderful is the God in Whom we believe. He will not fail us! He is the God of Elijah, supplying our every need. He is a great God! I praise the Lord that I believe in a Supreme Being who is "able to do exceeding abundantly above all that we ask or think, according to the power that worketh in us" (Ephesians 3:20). "But my God shall supply all your need according to His riches in glory by Christ Jesus" (Philippians 4:19).

From that experience, the Lord taught me that physical hunger is bad, but spiritual hunger is worse. Millions are dying for lack of spiritual food. I want to give the living bread to those who are dying so that they can eat and live.

5

Leaving School

I will never forget the day I had to leave school. I was 14 years old, and ever since I had given my heart to Jesus, five years before, I had been one of the top students in my class. That morning while I was getting ready to go to school, my father called me. "Son, you cannot go to school today," he said.

I looked up at him. He looked sad.

"Why?" I asked.

"Yesterday, your principal sent home a letter. If I do not pay your school fees, I cannot send you to school anymore."

"Father, why don't you give me the money?" I asked. "You know how much I love school."

Then my father did something I had never seen before. He turned his face to the wall and began to cry. "I know, son," he said. "But I don't have the money."

When I saw him crying, I began crying, too. I quickly said, "Don't cry, Father. It is all right. I don't have to go to school. I'll do whatever you say."

My father turned to me, wiped his eyes, smiled faintly and patted me on the back. "Perhaps," he said, "We can find you a job in one of the shops in Old Jerusalem so you can earn a few piasters."

We left our home in the Valley of Hinnom and walked north through the high arching gate into the Old City of Jerusalem. We went first to the carpenter shop, which was owned by a member of our church, but he said that he did not have much work and could not hire me. Then we went to the goldsmith's shop. A dear Christian brother owned this shop, and I had worked there before, after school and on Saturdays. But he did not need help either.

So we went to the shoemaker's shop, near King David's pool. It was a dark, cramped shop with only one window. The owner was a rough man; a cigarette hung out of his mouth. But he was willing to take me on. "Let him sit here," the cobbler said, "and we will see what he can do."

I sat on a little stool as tears rolled down my cheeks. I did not want to be in this dark, smoke-filled shop. I wanted to be in school. I steeled myself and thought, *Now I must learn to be a shoemaker.* From that day forward I sat on that stool six days a week, 12 hours a day, from eight in the morning until eight at night. At first, I tried to keep up on my studies, but I worked such long hours that it was impossible. Many times I saw other children going to school, and I cried because I could not join them.

I only earned 50 piasters a week, which was equal to half a British pound. It does not sound like much money, but back then, with one piaster we could buy three loaves of fresh bread. So my small salary was enough to buy bread for my entire family.

Before I had to leave school, I used to rise every day at 4:00 A.M. and go to the baker's, hoping to buy yesterday's bread. If they had any loaves left from the day before, they would sell me four loaves for a piaster. But if all the old bread was gone, I had to buy fresh bread, three loaves for a piaster. I would arrive just as the shop was opening, buy bread and carry it home. Then I would go back to bed and sleep for a few more hours before I had to get up for school.

But now I was working. The shopkeeper showed me how to work with leather and within a few weeks I was making shoes. Soon my hands were stained brown from the leather dyes. They looked dirty, so I hid them in my pockets whenever I was in public.

I was a very good shoemaker. All the customers wanted me to make their shoes. I think I could have become rich making shoes, but God had other plans.

One day I was working at my low table, with the New Testament open before me. As I sewed shoes with both hands, I read. My boss came in. He snatched the Testament from the table and threw it to the ground, then slapped me so hard I nearly fell from the stool.

"Don't you bring that book here again," he shouted.

I began to cry. I picked up the Testament. I kissed it and put it in the breast pocket of my shirt and picked up my work. I wept bitterly. "Lord," I said, "I can't even read the Bible here."

Exactly three days later, God set me free from that shop.

That day I was alone in the shop during the noon hour. Everyone else had gone out to eat. I was in the back of the shop, in a small room where the sun never shone, stitching shoes. It was dark and damp back there, lit only by a weak gaslight. Suddenly I heard the voice of God saying, "Samuel, Samuel! Leave everything and follow Me, and I will make you a fisher of men."

The voice was audible, just like any other voice I had heard. I was so startled; I dropped the shoe I was sewing. *Who is speaking to me?* I wondered, but instantly I knew. It was the Lord.

"Lord," I said, "I cannot be a preacher. I had to leave school at 14 and I have no money to go back."

Again the voice came as just clearly as the first time, "Samuel, Samuel! Leave everything and follow Me and I will make you a fisher of men."

I heard the voice just as clearly as I have heard anyone's voice. I knew in my heart that God was calling me to be a preacher of the Word. I knelt weeping and said, "All right, Lord, I cannot disobey this heavenly call. I will obey. I will go anywhere. I will do anything.

If You have called me—and I know You have—I will believe You can supply my needs. Open the way, do miracles, do the impossible, and give me enough education that I might become an effective minister of Your Word."

I stood up, right in the middle of the day, and walked out of the shop and went home.

When my mother saw me she asked, "Why are you home in the middle of the day?"

"Mother," I said, "I am not going to work in that shop anymore."

My mother asked again, "What happened?"

I didn't know what to say to her, so I did not reply. Hearing God's voice audibly had been such a powerful experience. I wanted to be alone with God, to get closer to Him and confirm my calling. I decided to pray and fast until I was certain of God's call. For three days I fasted and prayed, and God reassured me.

But my mother, like all mothers, wanted me to eat. After three days, she tried to force me to eat.

"Mother," I told her, "please stop pressuring me."

"But why aren't you eating, Samuel?" she asked.

"It is all right, Mother. I can't eat. Do not force me. I am having a wonderful time with the Lord."

At this my mother went into her bedroom and closed the door.

I tiptoed over and put my ear to the door. I heard her praying, "Lord Jesus, I sense that You are doing something in Samuel's heart. You know, Lord, that we have always wanted him to be a preacher, but we did not have enough money to keep him in school. We had to put him to work as a shoemaker, but Lord, we gave him to You before his birth. We named him Samuel, 'Servant of the Lord,' so he could be a minister of Your Word. Lord, if You are calling him to be a preacher, help him obey Your call."

When I heard my mother praying, I rejoiced. "Thank you, Lord," I prayed, "that I was given to You before my birth. I was named Samuel. Help me fulfill my name and become a preacher."

After this time of fasting, I began to preach the Word. I could feel the Spirit working miracles in me.

* * *

Over the last 50 years, I have taken many people on tours of the Holy Land. In the beginning, I took people from Beirut, but now I take people from all over the world. On every tour, I take my group into the Old City of Jerusalem to my old shoe shop. I have taken so many tour groups to that spot, that all the shopkeepers know me. I stand in front of the shop, while my tour group gathers round me, and I tell them, "This is the door where I came out, under the call of God, at the age of 16. From this door, I have gone to 127 countries all over the world."

6

Bible School

After I left the cobbler's shop, I began to pray that God would lead and guide me and open the door for me to go to Bible school. There were no Bible schools where I lived, so I hoped that someone would send me to school in another land. I went up to every missionary I met and every preacher that came to our church, and told them, "I've heard the voice of the Lord. He has called me to be a preacher." Each patted me on the back and said, "That is very good. God bless you." But no one helped me. I began to lose hope that anyone would send a poor boy like me to Bible school. So I began to pray that God would open a Bible school in Jerusalem. I told God, "I believe You can do it!"

Then devil came close to me to tempt me, and said, "Samuel, you are being very foolish. Do you really think God will open a Bible school in Jerusalem just for you?"

I said to the devil, "You keep quiet. I am not speaking to you. I am praying to Jesus."

The devil left me and I continued to pray asking, "Lord, open a Bible school in Jerusalem."

After three months of praying, a dear brother came to me and said, "Samuel, have you heard the news? The Christian and Missionary Alliance is opening a Bible school in Jerusalem."

I was so excited. I raced back to my secret corner where I had spent hours in the presence of the Lord and knelt there to pray, but before I started I said to the devil, "Did you hear that? The Lord has opened a Bible school in Jerusalem!"

Then I prayed, thanking God, saying, "Lord, I thank You for opening a Bible school in Jerusalem."

When I finished thanking God, I went back to my friend and asked him, "Tell me more about this school. What are the requirements?"

He looked at me sadly and said, "Samuel, I do not think you can go. There are three conditions: You must be a high school graduate. Then you must pay 60 Palestinian pounds if you want to be a boarding student. But even if you manage these two, the third condition is impossible. You must be 21 years old!"

Lord, I thought, *I do not have a high school education, but You can give that to me right now, from heaven. Lord, I do not have the money, but You are a rich Lord. Surely You can supply 60 pounds. Lord, I know You can do all these things. But Lord, how can You make me 21 when I am only 16?* I could not figure this problem out, but I said, "Lord, I believe that You are able to do the impossible."

I hurried home and put on my long trousers. I had only one pair, but I wanted to look as old as possible. Then I went to the school and knocked on the door. The school was on Prophet Street, just north of the high stone walls that surrounded the Old City. The dean opened the door. I looked up and up at him. I was five feet seven inches tall, and he was six foot six inches tall. He towered over me. He invited me in and looked me up and down as if to measure me. He introduced himself as Rev. Leigh Irish and asked me, "What is your name?" He was an American from Georgia and he had a strong southern accent, which was a little hard to understand.

I had studied English in elementary school and had often gone up to missionaries and guest speakers from America to try to speak with them, but I knew very little English.

"Samuel Doctorian," I answered.

"What can I do for you, Samuel?" he asked. I thought, *You can do many things if you want to.* But I said, "Rev. Irish, God has called me to be a preacher. God has burdened me to pray for a Bible school and I believe this school is the answer to my prayers. I have come to enroll as a student. Please accept me."

Rev. Irish looked me over, from head to foot. He rubbed his bald head, then asked the first and hardest question, "How old are you?"

I had to tell the truth. "I am 16." All the while I was praying in my heart, *Lord, help him say "yes." Help him say "yes!"*

He rubbed his head and looked me over again. "Samuel," he said, "I have a strange feeling we are going accept you as a special student."

"Thank you, Rev. Irish!" I cried. Then I ran out of the door before he could ask the other two questions. The hardest question had been answered. I ran home, "Mother, I am accepted! Praise the Lord, I will be a Bible school student!"

When my father heard the good news, he asked, "But Samuel, what about the 60 pounds? You cannot be a boarding student unless you have 60 pounds and I do not have it!"

"Father," I said, "God has called me. God gave me the faith to pray for a Bible school to open in Jerusalem. God has made a way for me to be accepted into this school. He will supply the need. Do not be concerned about this. I believe He will do it."

The first day of Bible school I awoke with such inexpressible joy in my heart. Before I left for school, I knelt with my father on my right and my mother on my left. Together we prayed and they dedicated me afresh to the Lord, saying, "Lord take him. Help him in the Bible school. Help him succeed and make him a soul winner."

I kissed my parents goodbye and went off to school. There were six other students in the school. Two married couples, a lady from Syria, and another young man. I was the youngest.

It was wonderful to be back in school. In the West there are many Bible schools, colleges and seminaries, but in all of Palestine, my school was the only Bible school. We were so thankful for our school.

7

Where is the Money?

After two weeks, the principal, Rev. Ralph Freid, called me in. "Samuel," he said, "we are very happy to have you as a student. You are eating here, studying here, sleeping here. But we must know Samuel, what about the money? Who will pay for your fee? If you like, we can divide it—20 now, 20 in three months, 20 in three more months."

I said to the principal, "Thank you for your kind offer, Brother, but I believe I am going to bring it in all at once."

"When?" he asked.

"Give me three days," I replied, "to pray about it."

"All right," he said.

I went back to my room and knelt in prayer. "Lord," I said, "I still need 60 pounds to pay for my Bible school. Lord, I need the money. You can supply it. You will supply it."

I prayed about it for three days, but at the end of that time I still did not have the money. Freid called me again. "Samuel, three days are over; we really need to know, who's paying for you? We are glad that you are here, and we believe you are called by God to be in this school, but what about the money? We would like to know."

I bit my lip to keep from crying because I had no answer. I begged Reverend Freid for one more day.

"Okay," he said.

I hurried back to my room and cried out to God. "Lord, I am not getting up from my knees until You give me this money. I am going to stay here until You give me Your assurance that You will provide." I continued to pray, even harder. "Lord, I believe that You can send that money right now from heaven, right now into my hand. I believe You, Lord. You are the God of miracles, the God of impossibilities . . . the God of supreme power. You can do it!"

The moment I began to pray with faith, I felt that I had the money. I said, "Thank You, Lord! I have the money!" I got up from my knees and wiped the tears from my eyes. I said, "Hallelujah! I have the money! But I do not know where it is."

I began to search my pockets to see if the money was there, but it was not there. "Lord," I said, "I do not feel like asking You for the money anymore because I feel I have it. But where is it, Lord? Please show me where it is. I believe that You have given it to me, but where is it?"

I went out of my room and began to walk back and forth in the garden. "I have the money," I said to myself, "but where is it?"

Just then our dormitory cook, Mrs. Bechar, came into the garden from Prophet Street. She had been to the market and her arms were full of bags. I went to help her carry her bags. "Samuel," she asked, "have you paid the Bible School yet?"

"No, Mrs. Bechar," I said.

"Praise the Lord!" she said, full of joy.

I was dumbfounded. "What do you mean, Sister? I said that I have not paid yet. What do you mean, 'Praise the Lord?'"

"Brother Samuel," she said, "Just now, while I was walking down Prophet Street, a man in the market put money in my hand. He said it was for the little Armenian boy in the Bible school.

"Who is this man?" I asked.

"He said that he has met you before, but that you do not know him well and he does not want you to know who he is."

"How much is it?" I asked.

"Sixty pounds," she replied. "Samuel, it is for your school fees!"

Words could not express the praise and thankfulness I felt toward my Lord. Mrs. Bechar took the money up to the principal. I did not wait for him to call me, I went right up to his office and knocked on the door.

Inside, he was counting the money. "Where did this money come from, Samuel?"

I answered, "I do not know. I prayed and the Lord supplied it! Hallelujah!"

To this day, I do not know who gave the money, but I know that God supplied it.

He is the same God today!

He is a God of miracles!

8

Baptized in the Holy Ghost

I had such close fellowship with the Lord while I was enrolled in the Bible school in Jerusalem. It was there that I learned to give my studies to God. I would pray every time I opened a book, asking the Lord to help me learn. When I finished reading, I would close the book and ask God to help me remember what I had learned.

It was at the Bible school that I realized that I needed to be baptized. I obeyed and was baptized in the Jordan River in front of about 80 people from the Alliance church and many other friends. Twelve of us were baptized that day. I was the youngest and last to be baptized. On that day, I testified that I was willing to die for Jesus and to live for Him forever. It was a glorious day, one of the greatest days of my life.

Even after I was baptized in water, I felt that something was missing. I was serving the Lord. I was teaching the junior class in Sunday School, I was the treasurer for two societies and I had a burden for lost souls, but something was not quite right. The boys and girls in my Sunday school class looked up to me to guide their spiritual life, even though I was only a few years older than they were, but I felt that something was lacking in my heart.

Many times I felt that I had failed the Lord, and failed my friends, teachers and family. I would be bitter or proud or overcome with jealousy. I would feel a burning hatred toward someone who had wronged me. I was always going from brother to brother, morning and night, asking them to forgive me.

"Surely," I said to God one day, "You do not want me to live this way—troubled by wrong thoughts. Lord, I belong to You; why is it so hard for me to overcome my weaknesses?"

I did not know what I needed, but I knew to Whom I should go. I knew Who would bless my heart. I knelt in my little room, in the place where I had prayed for the 60 pounds. I wanted something better, something richer and deeper. I was praying and reading Acts, Chapter 2, where I read, "And the Holy Ghost came down." *What*, I wondered, *is this?*

"Lord," I said, "I do not remember anything like this ever happening to me. I believe I have Your Spirit within me because I am saved, but I have never had the Holy Spirit come on me with power the way it is described here in Your Word."

I was not so interested in the gifts of the Holy Spirit, such as tongues, or miracles, or healings, or prophecy. I simply wanted the Giver, the Holy Spirit Himself, to fall on me with power. I needed anointing. I needed unction from on high.

"Lord," I said, "I want Him. Let the Holy Spirit come upon me."

As soon as I prayed that prayer, the Spirit began to deal with me. He showed me things in my life that I needed to make right. Certain brothers I had grieved whom I needed to ask for forgiveness. Certain things for which I needed to make restitution. Certain books I had to burn. Certain pictures I must not keep. He began to cleanse me inside and out.

When you allow the Holy Spirit to work, He does His work perfectly. At once He began to show me what I had to do, the price I had to pay, and the consecration I must be willing to make to receive more of Him.

Lastly, He said to me, "Samuel, are you willing to love your enemies?" At first, I thought that I did not have any enemies, but then I remembered the people who had murdered my loved ones. When I heard the Holy Spirit asking me if I was willing to love them, I was afraid that if I said I was willing that He would say to me, "All right then, Samuel, I want you to go and preach to them to prove to Me that you really love them."

That thought terrified me. I knew I was not willing to go to the Muslims and tell them about Jesus. They had brutally murdered my loved ones! How could I love them?

Humanly speaking, it would not be possible. Those who are not yet sanctified cannot love their enemies unless they let God's refining fire burn up every dross of sin. For two weeks I struggled. Over and over again, I said to God, "Lord, do not ask me that question, but give me the Holy Spirit."

Every time God would say, "No. Not until you say that you are willing to love your enemies and hold nothing back."

I was praying to a living God. I was desperate for the Holy Spirit. Finally one day, thanks be to God, I shouted at the top of my voice, "I love them, Lord! I love them!"

I laid everything on the altar. At that moment, the fire fell. The Holy Spirit came in power on me just like He fell on the disciples that first Pentecost. The fire began to burn in my heart, my mind, my whole spirit and my body. The wonderful Holy Spirit began to take possession of me. When I was saved *I had the Spirit*, but now *the Spirit had me*. What a difference! What a wonderful experience!

All this happened on April 30, 1946. I was 16 years old and had only been in Bible school seven months. Once the Holy Spirit came upon me, my life was changed. My hands were different. My eyes were different. My whole being was lost in Christ. I could truly say, "I am crucified with Christ: nevertheless I live; yet not I, but Christ liveth in me. . ." (Galatians 2:20).

Looking back, I am thankful that I had not heard of the baptism of the Holy Spirit before I experienced it. In the west there are so many controversial arguments about the Baptism of the Holy Spirit; so many doctrinal differences, denominational barriers, and heartbreaks. I am glad that I did not know about all these troubles before the Holy Spirit fell on me. Let me tell you something: the more you argue about the Holy Spirit, the more you grieve Him. Today when people want to argue with me about the Holy Spirit, I simply tell them, "I do not know what you think about this subject, but I know what I have. It is a great blessing to my soul. I cannot deny it. God has done a great work in my heart."

You can call it a "baptism," or you can call it "entire sanctification," or you can call it "consecration"—I do not care what you call it. But get the blessing. That is what the church of Christ needs today. Why should you live a Christian life that is so poor when you can be so rich? Why should you stay away from Pentecostal experience because some people have misrepresented Pentecost?

I am so grateful to have had this second experience of God. You can too. It will change your whole spiritual life. You see everything clearly. You are one with Jesus—full of the Holy Ghost. You have the gifts of God. You have the fruits of the Spirit within you. It is a tremendous experience.

* * *

The Lord Jesus, Who saved me, also baptized me with the Holy Ghost and with fire, and that fire has been burning in my life ever since that day on Prophet Street in Jerusalem. This power of the Holy Spirit that the Bible speaks about is not physical power. It is power to be an effective witness. It is power to win souls to Christ. It is power to love your enemies. It is power to live like Christ Jesus. It is power to overcome the devil and sin.

The Holy Spirit was promised by the Father; He was promised by Jesus. He is biblical truth. He is practical; He is personal, and this experience of being filled to overflowing can happen to you while you are reading these lines. Allow Him to come in. It is the will of God. It is the call of God. It is the work of God that sanctifies you—your whole body, your soul and your spirit so that all will be preserved blameless for the coming of the Lord Jesus Christ. "For faithful is He that calleth you, who also will do it" (I Thessalonians 5:24).

It is the prayer of Jesus, the command of Jesus, that you might receive the power of the Holy Spirit. The Spirit wants to come and dwell in you so He can make you His holy temple. Are you willing to pay the price? Have you let the Holy Spirit fall on you?

You can receive the baptism of the Holy Spirit and you will know the difference. You will be different, changed, from the moment you receive the blessings of holiness. Allow Him to take full charge of your life, and you will be fruitful. You will become a great blessing and be a powerful witness.

Brothers and sisters, seek the second touch. Cross the second crossing. Let the second experience be yours. Let this rich grace of God happen to you. You will be richly restored, and see everything clearly.

9

To Scotland

While I was a student in the Bible school in Jerusalem, an Irish missionary to Jerusalem, Rev. Russell, told me about a Nazarene school in Scotland. He said that the Nazarenes would pay my way if I would go. The Nazarenes are the largest denomination in the Wesleyan-Arminian tradition, a tradition that believes that God gives eternal life to those who respond in faith. My family had been Nazarenes ever since we had moved to Jerusalem.

I was very grateful for my Bible school in Jerusalem. I was thankful for the professors who had taught me to pray through my difficulties, who prayed for me, and who taught me God's Word. But I knew God was leading me to Scotland. The dean of the Bible school, the tall man who had accepted me, spent two hours trying to persuade me to stay in Jerusalem, but I was convinced—I had such a strong witness in my spirit—that God was saying, "Go to Scotland."

I was only 17 years old, but I said goodbye to my father, my mother, my three brothers, and my two sisters and got on a boat for Marseilles, France. My father did not have enough money to buy me a suitcase. What little I had, I put in a sheet and carried in a bundle on my back.

The Nazarenes paid my ship and train fare, about 50 pounds sterling, but I had no money for food. On the ship to Marseilles, they fed us, but once I left the boat, I had no food, nor any money to buy food. I fasted and prayed as I rode in the train from Marseilles to Paris, then on to Calais. In Calais the train was loaded onto a ferry and in this way we crossed the English Channel. Once we landed in Dover, we continued to London, and then Scotland. I traveled day and night without eating. In England, a young man across from me opened a large packet of sandwiches and ate them all, without offering me a morsel. I was so hungry. For three days and nights I had nothing to eat. But I was determined to get to college to study and learn more about the love of God, and how to be a better preacher of the Word.

It was October, so as I traveled north the days got shorter. When the train pulled into the Glasgow station at nine o'clock in the morning, the skies were dark. At 10 it was still dark, cloudy, and overcast. This was my introduction to Scottish winters. For three months, I did not see the sun. The sky was always gray. For a boy from Israel, where we have three hundred days of bright sunshine a year, it seemed that the sun had all but vanished.

I waited for two hours for someone to pick me up from the train station. I had no money to buy anything, and I was famished after three and a half days without food. At last, a student came and took me to the college.

When I got to the college, the cook asked me, "Samuel, shall I prepare you an egg?"

I said, "That would be good."

"Would you like two eggs?"

"That would be better," I said, with a big smile.

That cook became a Scottish mother to me. She had no children and she would often invite me to visit her and her husband in their nearby home.

* * *

Two weeks after I arrived in Scotland, I got a letter from the dear dean in Jerusalem, the very one who had tried to persuade me to stay. "Samuel, surely God was leading you to leave. Just a few days after you left, war broke out between the Jews and the Arabs. We had to abandon the school and flee for our lives to Cyprus."

I believe that God opened that Bible school in Jerusalem just for me. The school was only open one year. Of all the people who attended the school, I am the only one who is still in the ministry. I believe the school was open that one year to train me and give me the experience I needed before I went out to preach the gospel. Truly this was an answer to prayer! God had not let me down! Glory be to God!

* * *

When I got to Scotland, my English was so limited that I was not able to share my faith or even say grace at the table. Every day during the four years that I was in Great Britain, I asked the Lord to teach me the language. I promised Him that I would use it only for His glory. He was the One who taught me how to speak English.

Every day God provided. Many, many times, when I was in desperate straits, the Lord worked miracles to meet my needs—even though I did not tell anyone I what I needed.

The closest Nazarene church was located outside of Glasgow in a place called Nit's Hill. We had to take a bus and a tram to get there. One day, I wanted to go to the Friday evening Young People's Society at church, but I did not have enough money for the bus fare. My fellow students came to me and said, "Come on, Samuel, let's go." But I said, "I cannot come."

They wondered why, but I did not tell them. Instead, I went to my room and fell to my knees, and cried out to God, "Lord, You have not brought me here to suffer like this. I want You to give me that shilling so I can go to church and worship You."

The Lord said, "I have given it, Samuel."

I got up, took my coat, walked downstairs and was headed out the door, when the cook shouted, "Samuel, Samuel!"

I stepped back inside. She handed me a letter with my name on it postmarked Ayrshire.

I opened the letter, and, praise the Lord, there were 10 shillings inside! A lady from Ayrshire said that the Spirit led her to send the 10 shillings to the Armenian boy who had just arrived from Jerusalem. She had never seen me, nor I her, but she had sent the money so the Lord might bless me and use me for His glory!

I ran out the door and down the hill to the bus stop where the other students were still waiting for the bus.

I had asked the Lord for one shilling and He had given me 10.

The Filson family, the family that sent me those 10 shillings, continued to send me small bills during the four years I was in Scotland. They were a great blessing to me. Even after I left Scotland, I continued to get letters from them with money to support my ministry in the Middle East.

*   *   *

Another time I was at a Nazarene church in Uddingston, Scotland, attending the Sunday evening service when God supplied my need once again. I had gone to hear one of my favorite professors preach. The roundtrip bus fare cost two and a half shillings—half a crown. I had that much in my pocket, but during the service they took an offering, and I put my half-crown in the offering plate. *Now, I thought, I will have to walk for hours on the dark road to get back to the college because I haven't any money for the bus.*

As people were leaving the church I helped an old lady down the aisle. As she went out the door, she turned to thank me, and placed a half-crown in my hand. "God bless you, son," she said. It was exactly what I needed to get back to college. Again God had provided.

10

Providential Lunch

During my third year in Seminary, four of us students decided to go from city to city preaching the Gospel during our Christmas holiday. We traveled all over the countryside between London and Glasgow singing our theme song:

We'll follow Him together, wherever He leads.
By streams of living water our souls He doth feed.
Whatever is the conflict, He'll meet our every need.
We'll follow him together, wherever He leads.

We sang in the meetings, on trains and buses, and even as we walked along the road. My friend and fellow student, John Crouch, would preach; I sang solos and gave my testimony. In the hopes of attracting more students to the college, all of us testified as to how the Lord had led us to the school.

The other three decided I should be the group's treasurer. I could not imagine why. I had no money, but they told me, "We figure you have more faith than we do." So I kept the accounts: how much money came in, what we spent, and where we ate. Every day we prayed that God would supply our daily bread.

One day we were in the city of Derby at noon. We were hungry. In a few hours, we were going to take the train to the next city where we would hold an evangelistic meeting that night, but meanwhile we were on our own. We had only half a crown among us. We began to walk around the town looking for a place to eat. We looked longingly at the menu posted outside a fine restaurant. The food sounded delicious, but it was too expensive. We walked away.

The more we walked, the hungrier we became. Suddenly, my heart was filled with faith. I had an unshakable assurance that God knew our need and would supply. "Brothers," I said, "Let's go back to that beautiful restaurant and eat whatever our hearts desire. The Lord will provide."

The other three men began to laugh. "Samuel," one said. "Do you know what you are saying?"

"I have such faith. I know God is going to do a wonder."

"If we don't pay," one of the brothers said, "we will be in big trouble. We might end up washing dishes, or worse!"

"Don't tell me words of doubt. I have strong faith that the Lord will provide for us."

We walked back to the restaurant. The main floor was crowded, so they led us upstairs. There was only one table up there, and there was a woman enjoying her meal at the far end. We sat at the other end of the table.

The brothers looked at the menu, leaned forward, and whispered, "Samuel, what should we order?"

"Anything your heart desires," I said, confidant that God would provide.

My friends were so hungry that they did not need much encouragement. They ordered all kinds of meats, potatoes, vegetables, and pies. The waiter brought the food, and one of the brothers, a young man named Alec Jones started to eat. "Alec, we have not prayed yet," I reminded him.

I began to pray, thanking God for the food. I thanked God for bringing us to that restaurant and thanked Him for blessing us. Then I closed the prayer in Jesus' name and took up my fork.

While I was praying, I noticed that the lady at the end of the table had stopped eating.

Before I could take a bite, the lady asked, "Excuse me, who are you?"

I answered, "I'm from Jerusalem and these young men are from different cities in England. We are students at a Bible school in Scotland. Right now, we are traveling and serving the Lord." I wanted to start eating, but she had another question, and another question, and another question. I began to wonder, *Is this lady ever going to stop asking questions so I can eat?*

Then she said to me, "Will you excuse me?" She signaled the waiter and said, "Can I have their bill? I want to buy lunch for these four young men."

The moment she said that, the other three students froze, forks in midair. One was so startled that he dropped his fork. They couldn't believe what was happening.

I was so touched and moved by the Lord. I told the lady, "We four are sitting here, eating by faith, trusting God to supply our needs."

Her eyes filled with tears, and with great joy she went and paid the bill. We rejoiced to see how the Lord honored our faith and supplied the money for our food. Praise His name!

11

Preaching in Great Britain

While in Great Britain, I was privileged to preach in many churches in England, Scotland, and Ireland. Every Sunday, I was invited to testify and sing, so while I was still a student I would go out to preach during my school holidays. I crossed the Irish Sea 22 times. Everybody wanted me to sing a song called Mother's Prayer. It went like this:

> I never can forget the day,
> I heard my mother kindly say,
> "You're leaving now my tender care;
> Remember, child, your mother's prayer."

The song moved everyone to tears, and I cried, too. I sang this song all over Ireland where the women cried so hard that I said I would never sing that song again!

As part of our seminary training, we were assigned student pastorates. I was assigned to a church in Ireland for three months. During that time, God's wonderful power was manifested. My last year in seminary, I pastored a church in Dunfermline, the ancient capital of Scotland across the *Firth of Forth*, or Forth River from Edinburgh. In that church, God richly blessed us the 52 Sundays that I was there. Almost every Sunday, souls came to the altar to be saved. The church grew Sunday after Sunday. We felt the blessings of the Lord resting on our meetings. I praise God for all the blessings in that church! I grew in grace and became more and more comfortable with my responsibilities as the year progressed.

*   *   *

After I graduated, I traveled full time. I remember a beautiful little town in Scotland called Ardrosan, on the Scottish sea in the eastern part of the country. As you may know, the Scots are not easily shaken or moved. They are quite stoic. I had been holding evangelistic crusades in Dundee in the North and was on my way to Ardrosan, when I met a preacher named Cyril who had been one of my fellow students at the college. He was also the son of the district superintendent. I asked him, "Cyril, where were you preaching last week?"

"Ardrosan," he answered.

"Oh!" I said. "That's where I am going now."

"Ohhh," he said, shaking his head. "It was the most difficult city I have ever preached in. I will never go there again."

Oh my! I thought. *That's where I am headed. I will have to pray harder that the Lord will bless me in Ardrosan.*

In Ardrosan, we held one meeting, then two meetings, and then three meetings. During the third meeting, the Lord came with such power that the whole town was shaken. The mayor of Ardrosan came to the meeting. I will never forget his white hair. When I gave the altar call, he came forward and dedicated his life to the Lord. He gave me the key to the city and granted me freedom to do whatever I wanted when visiting.

I went to the Salvation Army, and told them, "I need your band. I need every one of you." They all joined in. We marched through the city. The Lord moved so mightily that after one week, I stayed another week. Then another; and another week until the whole town was shaken with the mighty power of the Holy Ghost.

We held a baptismal service in the nearby sea. The Scottish Sea is very cold, but we went down to the sea and baptized new converts to the faith. The next day, the front page of the Scottish newspaper reported: "Preacher from Jerusalem Baptizes Scottish Candidates." So many Scottish souls got saved. It was a great revival.

I am still friends with the pastor of that church in Androsen. For many years he was the director of the Church of the Nazarene in Europe and the Middle East.

* * *

Another time when I was traveling, I stayed at the home of some dear friends, Jim and Liberty Osmand. He was British; she was Armenian. I was invited to their wedding while I was in seminary because I was one of the few Armenians in that part of Scotland. After they married, they had a child, but the child did not live long. A little later, they had twins, but one died a few hours after birth and the other one died a few days later. It was heartbreaking.

One night after a meeting in a Methodist church, we were sharing around the kitchen table. They told me of their deep sorrow. The saddest part, Liberty said with tears in her eyes, was that the doctor said there was no hope for another baby. "I am so sorry I've lost those three, but the worst is that I cannot have any more. I would love to have a child."

I felt so sorry for them. I prayed with them, then, at about 11 o'clock, I went up to bed. I fell on my knees to pray at the side of the bed. As I prayed, an angel of the Lord came into the room and stood before me. A bright light emanated from him. He had a glorious face and a wonderful smile. He held a scroll, which he opened and read, "Go and tell my daughter. I shall give her a son next year."

You can imagine my joy. I grabbed my robe and ran down the stairs. Brother Jim and his dear wife were still in the kitchen, talking quietly and crying.

"Liberty, I have a message for you! Just now the Lord sent an angel into my room. "

"An angel? Right here?"

"Yes. He came into my room while I was praying and gave me a message for you: 'Next year at this time, you will have a son!'"

We stayed up late that night, rejoicing and praising the Lord for this glorious message. Exactly a year later a boy was born.

Eighteen years later, I met that precious son. I was back in England, preaching at a convention where Brother Jim was serving as a counselor and speaker. They were so happy to see me, but they were even happier to introduce me to their son, their precious one. How thrilling it was to see him, hug him and kiss his cheeks. The best part is that he was a dedicated Christian, who had given his life to the Lord. I praise God for the glorious and wonderful fulfillment of the message the angel brought into that bedroom so many years before.

12

Revival and Ordination

During my student days, I was often troubled by a lack of zeal among my fellow students. Most of them were studying hard, intently focused on the academic aspects of seminary, but I wanted more than just an education—more than head knowledge. I wanted the anointing of the Holy Ghost. I wanted to know God, not just learn about Him. I longed for revival. My fellow students seemed lukewarm, without passion for God or a heart for the lost.

I prayed fervently that God would touch the student body. I prayed for revival, but revival did not come. One night I got so discouraged, so frustrated, that I said to the Lord, "Bring revival or let me die! I want to die tonight, Lord. Unless You bring revival, take my life!"

I went to bed believing that I would die. In the morning, when I opened my eyes, and I realized that I was very much alive, I got angry. I complained, "Lord, I told You! Revival or take my life!"

He said, "Would you say that again?"

"Revival or take my life!"

"Well, I didn't take your life," He answered, "so what does that mean?"

"Ohhh!" I said with excitement. "Then revival is coming!"

Then the Lord revived me. I was on fire. I was able to let go of all the anger and frustration and receive a fresh anointing from the Holy Spirit. That spirit of revival began to burn in me. It is still burning in me from that day forward until today.

*   *   *

People often ask me what I mean by the word "revival." The term re-vival, the word itself, means to vitalize again something that used to be on fire, but it has cooled off—become lukewarm. People have backslidden. The Holy Spirit has been grieved. Souls are not getting saved. There is no conviction in the meetings when there is ministry of the Word of God. And the church has become full of dry, fruitless believers. There is no glory anymore in their spiritual lives, no power, no anointing. During revival there is an awakening to the things of God. There is a visitation of God. Revival does not come to sinners who have never been saved. Revival comes to believers. Later, unbelievers come to the Lord, but first the church must be revived.

*   *   *

After I graduated, I was ordained in Scotland by Dr. J.B. Williamson, one of the General Superintendents of the Nazarene Church, in Parkhead Church in Glasgow, the oldest Nazarene church in Great Britain. I was only 21 years old—the youngest person to be ordained in the history of the British Nazarene Church. I will never forget when I fell on my knees and 32 ministers laid hands on me, ordaining me.

It nearly didn't happen. The day before, I met with the board of examiners, who asked me question after question. I could answer every one. In the whole British Isles, I was winning more souls to the Lord than any other preacher. I had graduated from seminary. I had done my pastoral duty. I had done everything they required for ordination.

When they finished questioning me they said, "Samuel, we love you. We would love to ordain you. But if we don't ordain you this year, will you be discouraged? You are so young!"

"No," I said, my voice steady. "I am ordained already."

"Ordained already? Who ordained you?" they asked in disbelief.

"The One who called me," I replied. "John 15:16 says, 'Ye have not chosen me, but I have chosen you and ordained you, that ye should go and bring forth fruit and that your fruit should remain: that whatsoever ye shall ask of the Father in my name, he may give it you.' God has ordained me."

The examiners looked at each other and then at me. Then they asked me to leave the room.

"All right," I said. "Thank you, gentlemen."

That night in the chapel, the board of examiners announced that they had decided to ordain five people. They began reading the names. They read four names. I was sitting in the back of the church listening for my name. They read the fifth name: "Samuel Doctorian."

I began to cry. I would be ordained tomorrow!

On Easter Monday, 1951, the five of us—including my dear friend John Crouch and me—knelt together and were ordained for the ministry.

Later, I got hold of one of those five brothers and asked them, "What made you change your mind?"

He said, "After you left the room we said to one another, 'If the Lord has ordained him, we'd better do it, too.'"

Hallelujah! Hallelujah!

I believe in apostolic succession by ordination. I believe in the laying on of hands by the presbytery. I believe it is a tremendous blessing from the time of the Apostles all the way to our general superintendent. They lay hands on us and ordain us to the ministry, but I tell you, if the Lord has not done the ordination, man's ordination will not avail. It is just a diploma. But if God has ordained, and the church confirms that ordination, then there is a tremendous blessing from God.

* * *

My four years in seminary were a wonderful time. We enjoyed such close fellowship at the college and we saw many miracles during this time. God supplied my every need—spiritually, physically, and materially. He did not fail me. He is the same Lord today—a God of miracles. I give Him all the glory. I am what I am, only by His grace.

13

Call to the Middle East

While I was still a student in the Nazarene College I heard God telling me that I was His chosen vessel to bring revival to the Middle East. I had a tremendous burden in my soul for evangelism. I sensed that God was calling me to a wider field where I could preach the Gospel to hundreds and thousands of people.

Some of my fellow students thought I was being presumptuous. After all, wasn't I the youngest student in my class? They would say, "Who does he think he is? He thinks he is going to bring revival to the Middle East!" But one student, John Crouch, believed that this was God's call.

I had enjoyed my time in Great Britain, but I still felt a call to the Middle East. Sometimes I got discouraged and wanted to escape this call. I knew that the Middle Eastern countries were some of the hardest countries of the world. I was tempted to seek a comfortable church in Britain, or even America, but deep in my heart I knew that God was calling me back to the Middle East.

One day, I was in the train on my way to Perth. Back then the trains had compartments that seated about six people in two rows facing each other, like a little room. I had a compartment all to myself, so I was having a grand time, singing praises to God. The conductor opened the door and stepped in to check my ticket.

"You seem happy," he said.

"I am so happy," I answered. "I am praising the Lord. My sins are forgiven. I'm washed in the blood of the Lamb."

He punched my ticket quickly and walked right out.

I was having a wonderful time. After he left I started singing again. I was having such a good time and then, suddenly, Jesus appeared in front of me.

He asked me, "Samuel, where are you going?"

"To Perth, Lord."

"Samuel, where are you going?"

"Lord," I said, "I just told you. I am going to Perth."

He said, "Samuel, I brought you to Scotland. You're ready now. You have finished your college. I helped you finish it successfully. You have been a blessing here, for I have blessed you. I supplied your every need. But now, Samuel, I want you to go back to your own people in the Middle East and fulfill your promise to Me to reach your people, the Armenians, the Arabs, and the Muslims, whom you promised you would love. Go, Samuel."

I fell on my knees in the compartment of the train and wept before God. I made my vow. I dropped everything. I sat down one morning and I wrote 33 letters by hand, canceling all of my upcoming speaking engagements, which were booked for months ahead.

"I am going back," I said. "I am going to obey the Lord."

* * *

On the way back to Jerusalem, I stopped off at my old seminary in Hurlet for one night. That night at suppertime, I said to the student body, "As you know, I am leaving to take the Gospel to the Middle East, but I am still very burdened for revival in Great Britain. Before I leave in the morning, I want to pray for revival. I am going to spend all night in prayer. Anybody who wants to join me is welcome. We will be meeting in the prayer room."

Some of the students were excited, and said, "Samuel, we'll join you." Others wished me well, but did not want to come.

About nine o'clock we began to pray. One by one students joined us. Those who had gone back to their dormitories had fallen under the conviction of the Holy Ghost. No one could sleep, so they came. By 10 o'clock every student in the college was in the prayer room.

By 11 o'clock, we were shouting praises to God on our knees with our faces to the ground. We could feel the fire of the Holy Ghost burning in every heart. I was rejoicing to see what God was doing in us. By midnight, we were on fire.

At one o'clock in the morning, one of our professors, Dr. Kenneth Grider, appeared in the door of the prayer room. "What's going on?" he asked. "What is all this noise and commotion coming from the prayer room?"

As soon as he got the words out of his mouth, he fell to the floor under the power of God and began to cry. Fifteen minutes later, he got up and left. I thought that he had had enough, but I was wrong. He had gone back home to awaken his wife. "Come and see," he told her. "The students are on fire." She got out of bed and got dressed, and a few minutes later they were both in the prayer room.

I was pacing back and forth, on fire for God. We could feel His presence. Suddenly Mrs. Grider began to cry. The Holy Ghost led me to her. I could feel the Holy Spirit of God burning within me. My tongue was on fire. My mind was on fire. My spirit was on fire. The Holy Ghost gave me a message for her: "I have heard your cry. I have heard your prayer. I shall fulfill the desire of your heart. Next year at this time, you shall have a child."

She screamed!

I shook, she startled me so. I was only 21 and knew very little about women or babies. I wondered if something was wrong.

Professor Grider turned to me with tears running down his face, "Samuel, what did you say?"

"I didn't say it," I replied. "The Holy Ghost said it. He took hold of my tongue. It's on fire. He gave that message."

"Samuel! For years we've been trying to have a baby. Yesterday we went to the top specialist in Scotland, and he told us, 'You cannot have children. Forget about it.' And now the Lord is saying NEXT YEAR YOU SHALL HAVE A CHILD?"

I could only nod mutely.

A year later, the Lord gave them a precious daughter.

They eventually had five children! Hallelujah! Five children!

Later that year, 1951, Dr. Grider wrote an article in the *Herald of Holiness,* the magazine of the Nazarene Church, with the headlines: "Fire Fell on Hurlet." In the article he described our night of prayer at Hurlet Nazarene College, in Scotland.

Years later when I was in Kansas, Professor Grider asked me to come home with him for dinner. By then he was a professor in a Nazarene Theological Seminary in Kansas City. He said, "Samuel, you must come to my home for supper. I want to gather the children together and have you tell them how the Spirit of God fell that night and you prophesied that we would have a baby."

* * *

I spent the next night in London, visiting my dear friend from seminary, John Crouch, then I took the train to Marseilles, where I boarded a ship for Beirut. As I traveled, I prayed that the Lord would make me a blessing in the Middle East. It was a joy to be going back.

14

Back in the Middle East

When I reached Beirut, I was privileged to preach to my own Armenian people at a camp meeting up in the mountains. The first message was glorious. I rejoiced that the Lord had brought me back to my country again.

From Beirut, I traveled to Jerusalem to see my parents. I entered the Old City through the Damascus Gate with my luggage on a donkey. The Damascus Gate is a tall portal more than 20 feet high, in the towering stone wall that surrounds the Old City. I wound through the narrow lanes looking for the place where my family now lived. I knew that the building was owned by a Coptic convent. They had been living there for four years, ever since war had broken out between the Israelis and the Arabs, shortly after I left for Scotland.

I was so thankful that they were alive. At one point, several years before, when I was still in Scotland, I had gone months without hearing from them. My letters had been returned to me stamped "occupants unknown, return to sender." I wept when I saw those letters. I was thousands of miles away, and I had no way of knowing if they were dead or alive. I tried to contact the Salvation Army to see if they knew where my family might be, but no one knew anything.

For six long months, I wondered if they were dead or alive. I knew the Arabs and Jews were fighting and that the Valley of Hinnom, where our home had been, had become a no-man's land, but nothing more.

One day in Scotland, I was playing the piano and singing, "It is well, it is well, with my soul." I was saying to myself, *If my parents are dead and my brothers and sisters, too, I will still serve the Lord faithfully, whatever the price.* The postman came with a letter for me. I recognized my father's handwriting. My heart leapt. The letter said, "Dear son, we have lost everything but Jesus. Our home has been bombed, and we have escaped with only what we could carry, but we are living by the grace of God." They were alive!

Now, four years later, I was walking down the narrow streets of the Christian quarter, looking for their address. When I found them, I was shocked. My entire family was crammed into one small room with only a few meager possessions. It broke my heart to see them living as refugees in such a sorry state.

My father said, "They destroyed our home, Samuel, but they were not able to destroy our faith in Jesus."

For four years they had waited, hoping every day that the fighting would stop and they would be able to go back and rebuild. I told my father, "Give it up! There is no hope you are going back there. You know the Bible better. The Bible says that one day Israel will take all of Jerusalem." Back then, in 1951, the Kingdom of Jordan ruled Old Jerusalem and Israel only had a small area to the west, but I knew from biblical prophecy that Israel would soon seize the Old City. "The day will come," I told my father, "when they will take this area also. It is all written in the Bible."

I squeezed into the small room where they were living and waited every day to hear where my denomination would place me. I was supposed to be assigned to the church in Jerusalem. Every day, I rose, shaved and dressed—no small task in such crowded conditions—and waited for my superintendent to confirm my assignment.

After 10 days they came to see me—the superintendent and Rev. Russell, the same Irish missionary who had sent me to Scotland. I had waited for days to see them, but they stayed only 10 minutes.

"We're glad, Samuel, you're back," they said. "We have not decided where to place you."

"I cancelled 33 meetings and came thousands of miles to lead the church in Jerusalem," I reminded them.

They looked at each other, and then Rev. Russell, said, "We'll let you know what we decide." Then they left.

They came back a few days later and told me that they had appointed another man to lead the church in Jerusalem. I was very disappointed. The man they had appointed was a carpenter with no training. I had traveled all the way to Scotland to go to seminary and all the way back to lead this church.

Every day that I had been back, I had preached in the Jerusalem church. The Holy Spirit was moving with power; the church was growing. It was crowded now. People were so happy to have me preaching. But my superiors wanted to send me away.

At first, they wanted me to go to the city of Zarqa, in Jordan, but there were only four Armenian families there. My parents refused to let me go.

"You're a young man of 21 and you're not married," my father said. "You can't go to a small town with so few Armenians." I did not want to go there either. It was not the call of God.

My superiors tried to force me to go, but I said, "No." Then they suggested Amman. The church in Amman was very small, but it was a larger city, the capital of Jordan, so we said, "Yes." I moved from Jerusalem to Amman and took my whole family with me.

I was paid only 20 Jordanian dinar. Out of that small salary, I had to pay 14 dinar in rent. With the six dinar that remained, we tried to live. It was impossible.

All the foreign missionaries were living in luxury: housed in the best part of Amman and driving beautiful cars, but the national workers like myself were living in poverty. I was discouraged. At times, I wondered, *Why had I come back?* But I knew the answer before I asked the question. I had come back to the Middle East because an angel of the Lord had told me to go back.

I was determined to overcome the hardships. I began preaching. At first, there were only four people, but I continued to preach and began to fast and pray. One day I spent the entire day—from seven in the morning until eight at night, 13 hours—on my knees in an old Roman amphitheater weeping for revival. Amman used to be one of the ancient Roman cities called Philadelphia. The amphitheater is in ruins, but I knelt there because it was a good place to be alone in the heart of the city. That whole day, I fasted from food and drink as I cried out to God amidst the jumbled stones.

I would get so full of the Holy Ghost, so drunk in the Spirit that I frightened people. One time when I was praying in my church, the Armenian Nazarene Church, one of my parishioners tapped me on my shoulder and said, "There is a Jordanian soldier outside who wants to talk to you."

I wondered, *What does he want?* I got up from my knees, but I was so lost in the Spirit, so drunk in the Spirit that as soon as he saw me he said, "I'll come back tomorrow." Something scared him. So much so, that he never came back and to this day I have no idea what he wanted.

I looked at his retreating form, shrugged my shoulders and went back inside to pray some more.

After many weeks in prayer, suddenly, tremendous revival came to Amman. God blessed us and we saw many souls saved. One of the converts from those meetings was on Trans World Radio every morning, for more than 30 years, preaching to thousands of Armenians all over the Middle East.

15

Marrying Naomi

It was during my time in Amman that I married Naomi. I knew I was going to marry her the first time I saw her, even though she was only 13. At my parents' request, I had stopped in Beirut on my way to Scotland to visit precious friends, the Pashgian family. Samuel Pashgian had been my father's best-man at my parents' wedding and his wife, Marie, had been my mother's matron of honor. I stayed in their home two weeks while I awaited my visa to Scotland. It was then that I met their daughter, Naomi. When I saw her, the Lord witnessed in my spirit, "Here is your wife." We were both so young, just 13 and 17, so I didn't tell anyone, but for four years I prayed that God would prepare the heart of Naomi Pashgian to be my future helpmate in the work of the Lord. When I came back from Scotland, I passed through Beirut and saw her again. Even though she was only 17, the Lord witnessed to me again, "This is your wife."

I didn't tell my parents until after we moved to Amman. Together, we went to Beirut to ask for Naomi's hand. She was willing to marry me, and we had the blessing of both sets of parents, so we got married in the Evangelical Church in Beirut. Naomi was 17 and I was 21. When I was in Scotland, I learned this saying: "Catch them young, train them well." It is not biblical, but I like it. Naomi has been a precious wife to me, and we have never regretted marrying so young. My father-in-law was well respected in the Christian community, so fourteen pastors from many different Armenian denominations attended our wedding. Then I took my dear wife to Amman. She was a born-again Christian and both of us had a burden for souls.

The Lord blessed our ministry in Amman. The Arabs heard about the revival among the Armenians and asked me to come preach to them. On the evenings when I did not have meetings in the Nazarene church, I preached in the Arab churches.

When my superintendent heard about this he came and said, "Samuel, you cannot preach in other churches. We are paying you your salary. You are a Nazarene." I said, "I am preaching there on the nights when I have no meetings in our church. What is wrong with that? God is blessing my meetings."

It was a difficult time. They would not listen to me, and we were living in poverty.

Six months after we married, Naomi and I were kneeling together in prayer when I heard the Lord saying to me, "Samuel, do not stay here, but go out and preach the Gospel everywhere I lead you. I will supply your needs." The Lord spoke to me through the verse, in I Samuel 14:7, which says, ". . . Do all that is in your heart. Go then; here I am with you, according to your heart" (NKJV).

"Lord," I said, "I will go."

Then I turned to my wife and said, "Naomi, what shall we do? The Lord is calling me. We must leave."

She turned to me and said, "What shall we do with all of our wedding gifts and furniture?"

"Listen, dear," I replied, "We will take one suitcase for you and one for me. We will leave everything else behind us. Let us go out for the salvation of souls."

I was glad when she said, "Yes, I am willing to go."

We left my family in Amman and boarded the train. Many Christians came to the train station to see us off. Naomi was pregnant with our firstborn, and all we knew was that once we got to Damascus, we were going to take the bus to my father-in-law's home in Beirut. We did not know where God would take us next. When people asked me, "Where are you going?" I replied, "I do not know!"

With tears flowing down our cheeks, we sang, "Anywhere with Jesus, I Can Safely Go," as the train pulled out of the station.

When we got to Beirut, my father-in-law was distressed to learn that I had quit my job. "I did not give my daughter to you to have her live like this!" he declared.

Later when revival came, he told me, "Samuel, I am glad you listened to the Holy Spirit."

*   *   *

As soon as we got to Beirut, I got an invitation to preach in Aleppo. Naomi and I went to Aleppo where I preached in the Armenian Brotherhood Church. I preached in five different Armenian churches in Aleppo. A dear brother who had been in Aleppo for 30 years testified that he had never seen such movements, such power manifested and such unity among the Christians. It was the greatest move of God in the city of Aleppo that any of us had ever seen. I gave all the glory to God. We had the largest evangelical church in the city, which seated over a thousand, packed to the doors every night for five solid weeks, as hungry souls listened to the Word and came forward to find the Lord at the altar.

16

Call to Egypt

From Syria, I went to Cyprus. For one month, I preached to the Armenians in the city of Nicosia. Then I heard the Holy Spirit say, "Go to Egypt."

"I don't know anybody in Egypt," I replied.

"You know Me, don't you?"

"Yes, Lord, I know You."

"Then go to Egypt."

I went to Egypt. I arrived in Cairo, the most populated city in all of Africa. Even back then, when I first went, there were two million people living in Cairo; now there are over 16 million. The city was packed with people. People jammed on to buses like Portuguese sardines. They would pile over each other to get on to the bus and even hang from the windows while the bus was going down the street. The whole city was crowded.

The Holy Ghost had said, "Go to Egypt," and I had gone, even though I was only 23 years old, and had very little money. Now I was at the British Airways office in the heart of Cairo saying to God, "Lord, here I am. What do You want me to do?"

I could feel the joy of the Holy Spirit, as I watched thousands of people going by on the streets and the overflowing buses lumbering down the road. Outside hundreds of horns were tooting at once. In Cairo, they believe the horn of the car is to be used. They blow their horns all the time, constantly, all together. I am not exaggerating. It made me smile to hear it. Toot. Toot. Toot. All over the city.

I was excited and happy, but I had no idea what I was supposed to do. Again I asked, "Lord, what do You want me to do?" I had a phone number of an American missionary in Cairo. I thought, *I'll call him and tell him that I'm in Egypt.*

The British Airways employees showed me the telephone. I found the missionary's number in my diary and called, but there was no answer. I called again. No answer. I called seven times in a period of two hours. No answer. I sat and prayed, *Please, Lord, guide me.* There was no answer from Him, either.

The British Airways employees were being very kind to me, but I could tell they were wondering, *Who is this young minister? What has he come here to do?*

Then the Spirit of God brought to my memory a name and address. I looked in my book and my eyes fell on that name, a dear brother called Toumayan living in a place called Faggala. I turned to the British Airways officer and said, "How far away is this city of Faggala?" He said. "That is not a city. That is a district here in Cairo. It is about 10 to 15 minutes by taxi, but don't go there."

"Why?" I asked.

"It is a very poor district. You don't want to go there. There are too many pickpockets. Too much crime. Too many robberies."

"I see. I wonder if you could help me find the telephone number?"

"Oh, there are no telephones in that district."

I decided to go anyway. I got a taxi. The driver put my bags in the trunk, and drove me to Faggala. It was a very poor area. The streets were terrible, full of holes. We pulled up in front of an old building. I checked the address. This was the place. I said to the taxi driver, "Don't go. Don't leave me alone; come with me."

I learned something that day. If you don't pay the taxi driver, he stays with you. He was a kind fellow, who knew I was a stranger, so he even carried my luggage up to the fourth floor of the building.

I found the name on the door and rang the bell. An old woman opened the door. As soon as she saw me, she raised her hands to heaven and shouted, "Praise the Lord! Welcome to Egypt, Brother Samuel!"

I was stunned. "Just a minute, Sister. How do you know that my name is Samuel?"

"The Holy Ghost told me, 'This is Samuel.'"

The Holy Ghost! I thought. "Marvelous," I said. I turned to the taxi driver, gave him his fare plus a good tip. "You can go now. I feel the Holy Ghost is here."

I entered the room, and asked, "Is this your home?"

She said, "No. I have only one room here. This apartment belongs to a lovely couple. They'll be here in half an hour."

"What do you do, Sister?"

"I fast and pray every day for revival in Egypt. Two weeks ago, I got a letter from Syria, about the revival in Aleppo, and daily I have cried out to God, 'Oh God, send Samuel to Egypt. Send Samuel to Egypt.'

"Just now I was on my knees when the doorbell rang, and the Holy Ghost said, 'Go, it is Samuel.' I got up from my knees, I came, and when I opened the door, the Holy Ghost said, 'This is Samuel.'"

I was astounded.

She was so happy to have me right there in front of her. She was praising God, too excited to sit down. She would walk about the apartment, and every five minutes, or so, she would circle back to me and say, "Oh, that's Brother Samuel." She acted as if she was not sure if she was seeing a vision or the real me.

In half an hour, the couple who owned the place came home. When they heard that I was there, the husband came straight to the living room, hugged me, kissed my cheeks, and said, "Welcome to this great country. We've been praying for you. Will you preach to us tonight?"

I said, "I've come for that."

That night I counted 19 people, including myself, that sister, that brother, his wife, and 14 others. The second meeting we had 40 people. At the third meeting, 80, then hundreds upon hundreds of hungry souls came filling the place to overflowing.

* * *

I went to Egypt to preach to the Armenians. I never thought of preaching to the Arab Egyptians, but God had something else in mind.

I was preaching to the Armenians in Cairo, when some Jewish Christians asked me to come preach to them. I went and preached to a small group, maybe 30 people on a Sunday afternoon. While I was preaching to those Jews in Cairo, two Egyptian Christians were outside the window listening. After the meeting one of them, a government official named Mousa Girgis, came to me and said, "We want to invite you to preach to our society." They had a small society of about one hundred people called the Soul Salvation Society.

"Sorry," I said. "I am too busy with my people. I don't have time to preach to Egyptians."

They begged me to come.

"Well," I hesitated. "I will give you one meeting."

The Soul Salvation Society was meeting for the express purpose of seeing souls come to Christ. They had started, by faith, in a little prayer room where the Lord had made their hearts burn for the salvation of souls. By faith, they had purchased a piece of land. God led me to those young people in such a marvelous way.

We started meeting with a few hundred people. I had meant to give them only one meeting. But God moved so mightily during that meeting that I could not stop. The one hundred became two hundred, three hundred, five hundred, until mighty revival came.

* * *

While I was in Egypt, Naomi was staying at her father's house in Beirut, pregnant with our first child. The whole time I was in Egypt, I was thinking, *My first child is about to be born, yet hundreds of souls are coming to the Lord. What shall I do? How can I leave this marvelous, spontaneous mighty move of God?*

I had told Naomi, "If the child is a boy, send me a telegram. If it is a girl, write me a letter." In the Middle East boys are favored over girls. Today I love my daughter with all my heart, she is precious! But back then I was young and so influenced by my culture. I was only 90 minutes away by plane, and I hoped to fly home as soon as the baby was born.

One evening, I was having dinner at the home of an Armenian brother when the postman came. It was a letter from Naomi. When I saw the letter, I assumed we had a girl, but when I opened the letter I saw that we had a boy! Naomi had done the opposite!

As I read that letter I wept with joy. It was torture to read Naomi's description of my little son's eyes, his lips, his little fingers and be so far away. I couldn't eat. I left the table, went to my bedroom, and fell on my knees.

"Lord," I said, "I am going home."

"Where?" He asked.

"Beirut."

"Why?"

"There is a boy, a precious boy! You have given me my first son."

"What about this revival here?"

"Lord, I know, but there is a son there!"

The Lord began to ask me, "What do you love? Your son or revival?"

"Both," I answered. "I love both."

"Which one do you love more?" the Lord asked me.

I paused. "I love revival, Lord," I replied.

"Then, Samuel," the Lord said, "you cannot go now. You must stay here until I tell you to go."

"All right, Lord," I replied. "I will do it."

I stayed in Egypt and continued working, winning souls to Christ. By the time I felt released to return to Beirut, my son was two months and 12 days old. Before I kissed his brow, I held him in my arms and dedicated him to the Lord. Then I kissed him. I was so glad to be holding him at last, but I was also thankful that God had given me many spiritual sons and daughters in Egypt.

Even today, I would give my life for my children at any time without hesitation. But I love revival even more, where sons and daughters are born into the kingdom of God, and saved for eternity.

17

Revival in Damascus

After a few days in Beirut with my wife and newborn son, I received an invitation to pastor a church in Damascus, Syria. I told them we would come if I could evangelize. They agreed and so I said I would come for one year. Immediately I began praying for revival to break out over the entire city of Damascus.

At first it was difficult. We worked hard for the Lord, praying and visiting homes and schools, telling people about the love of Jesus, but no one responded. I persevered. I wept before the Lord and I fasted.

I began praying with a Syrian pastor, a former Druz who was now a dedicated Christian. We were meeting in my home, fasting and praying for revival. Then a British missionary, Pauline Stammers, joined our group. Soon news of the prayer meeting spread to other churches and groups in Syria. Christians from other churches joined our prayer meeting. No one had invited them, but the Lord put the burden on their hearts. Soon people from many nations joined us in praying for revival.

The prayer meetings soon outgrew the living room. We had 20 people crammed in my house, so Pauline suggested that we move to the British and Syrian Mission. We had many wonderful prayer meetings in that location.

The spiritual climate began to change. For the first nine months that I was in Syria, only two souls came to the Lord. As we fasted and prayed, the spirit of prayer gripped hearts. Soon the Spirit of the Lord was stirring the hearts of ministers and Christian workers all over the city.

We started preaching the Word of the Lord, going from one church to another, until all the churches of every denomination were united together with one accord. More and more people joined our prayer meeting, including the pastor of the Presbyterian church, Pastor Mitri. He invited me to preach at his church. I don't think he realized what he had done. He had the largest church in Damascus, the Presbyterian Church, which was located in the heart of the city. We held meetings there for three months, every night. Christians in Damascus rededicated their lives to the Lord, and they were filled with the Spirit of the living God. The Lord was glorified and many precious souls came to know Him as their personal Savior.

* * *

The last three months that I spent in Damascus, hundreds of souls came to the Lord. Many of those who came to the Lord during that revival are still serving Him today. Many pastors serving in Damascus today came to Jesus during those meetings.

The man who led the Bible society in Damascus for many years, was a convert from one of those revival meetings. His story is amazing.

One night during our revival crusade, I was praying with people at the altar, going from one to the other, when the Holy Spirit prompted me to look up. In the back of the church, I saw a young man standing in the doorway. The Spirit of the Lord led me to leave the altar and go to this young man.

When I got to him, he looked angry, so angry that at first I thought he might strike me. I said "Good evening," but he did not answer. He only glowered. Then I asked, "What's your name?" He shouted angrily, "Najeeb Jarjour!"

I put my hand on his shoulder and began to pray, but he was so angry, that I honestly thought he might hit me on my face. I prayed anyway, with authority, "Lord, You love this young man! Touch him, bless him, convict him, and trouble him so much that he will not be able to sleep until he gives his life to You. In the name of Jesus." When I finished my prayer, he turned away, his face twisted in rage, muttering something I could not hear and left the church.

Some brothers came to me afterwards and said, "What did you say to that young man? He was blaspheming God and cursing you, when he left. What did you do?"

"I did nothing," I answered. I only prayed that the Lord would touch him and change his life. Who is he?" I asked. But nobody knew.

I went home, and began to pray for the angry young man. I asked, "Lord, was it wrong of me to pray like that? Should I not have said, 'Don't let him sleep until he gives his life to You?'"

The Lord said, "You did the right thing: you prayed the right prayer. Now go to sleep."

"Thank you Lord Jesus. Good night." I had wonderful sleep.

I later learned that the young man went home to his apartment and tried to study. He was a university student. He could not study. He tried book after book, but he could not focus. He was so troubled, so tired. So he went to bed.

He could not sleep. He tossed and turned in his bed, in the worst torture, feeling convicted and troubled.

He thought, *I wish I knew where that preacher is sleeping. I would like to go trouble him. I'd like to get my hands on him!*

Thank God he did not know where I was sleeping.

In the morning he got up, exhausted and began looking for me. He went to a grocery shop, and asked the owner, "Do you know where Samuel Doctorian lives?"

The grocer was a believer. He said, "Samuel was here, a few minutes ago, but he left. I think he went to see some people who live over there. The young man followed me there. When he got there, they told him that I had been there, but I had gone somewhere else. He followed me there, but again he couldn't find me.

Somebody told him that I might be in the prayer meeting at the British school. He went there. Pauline Stammers, my British missionary friend, opened the door and welcomed him inside. She could tell he was agitated.

"Why," she asked, "do you want to see Samuel Doctorian?"

"I couldn't sleep all night. I'm so troubled. It is his fault. It is because of his prayer!"

"You don't need Samuel," Pauline said. "You need the Lord!" She took him to the prayer meeting, and they fell on their knees together. Najeeb began to call on the name of the Lord to be saved.

It is amazing how the Holy Spirit guides us. I had been very busy that morning. I had come home for lunch. My wife was putting my lunch on the table. But I said to her, "I don't know why, but I've got a very strong feeling that I must go to the British school to the prayer group right away. I'll come back later for lunch."

I went to the prayer room. When I opened the door, who did I see? Najeeb on his knees, with Pauline Stammers next to him. He was giving his life to the Lord. When he heard the door open and close, he stopped praying, looked back and saw me. He got up came over and said, "If you had come few minutes ago, I would have beaten you, but now, I have given my heart to Jesus."

What a victory! I realized Najeeb was the same man I had prayed for the night before. We all prayed together, praising the Lord. I laid hands on Najeeb and asked God to bless him richly.

Years later, after he graduated from the university, Najeeb was in the Syrian Army. I heard he had become a captain and that he was stationed in Aleppo. I went all the way to Aleppo to see him. When he heard that I had come, he came running to see me, with a Bible in his hand.

"Najeeb," I said. "I came just to see you. How are you?"

"I was in a Bible study with a group of Syrian soldiers just now."

You can imagine my joy! I blessed him and went back home.

Sometime later, Najeeb became the director of a school. I went all the way to the school to see him. We hugged each other. I rejoiced to see how he was growing in grace. As the director he was leading many precious children to the Lord.

Najeeb said to me, "You'll be very happy with what I've done. I read the book by Billy Graham called *Peace with God*. I was very blessed by the book, so I wrote to the Billy Graham Association, and asked permission to translate it into Arabic. They quickly gave me permission. I translated the whole book and now I'm printing it in the Arabic language."

"I have found such peace with God," he continued. "I want the people of Syria to read this book and find peace with God, too."

You can imagine my great joy. God had saved him in Damascus, and now God was using him for His glory.

Later Najeeb met a lovely Christian girl, who had also been saved during the revival in Damascus, and they got married. They had a lovely family and all served the Lord.

Later Najeeb became the director of the Bible Society in Damascus.

The last time I saw Najeeb and his family, they visited me in Pennsylvania at a church where I was preaching. It was my great joy to see him, to see how he has grown in Christ! God is a great God. I give Him all the glory. In Jesus name, Amen!

18

The Death of a Boy & the Salvation of a Spiritualist

God did many wonders in Damascus during the short time that I was there. One that touched me deeply happened while I was in charge of a small elementary school with 41 boys and girls in first through fifth grade.

I was greatly burdened for the school children, so I set aside every morning for a week for a special crusade. On the fourth day, a teacher came to my office saying that the children were so touched by God that they were all crying. They want to give their lives to the Lord. I was thrilled.

I asked the whole class to come to my office. They fell on their knees and one by one they gave their lives to the Lord. You can imagine my joy!

That revival spirit soon spread to the other classes and within a few days the whole school had given their lives to the Lord.

Amongst them there was a wonderful boy, the only son of a very rich tailor in Damascus. The father was quite famous because he made suits for the president of Syria and many other government officials.

The family was Syrian Orthodox. When the father heard that his son had given his heart to Jesus, he got angry, and said, "I did not send my son to that school to become a religious fanatic!" He took him out of our school and enrolled him in an Orthodox school.

One day after school this precious boy of 12, ran from his new school all the way to my school just to tell me, "Nobody can separate me from Jesus. I love Jesus! I'm saved; don't worry about me!" Then he ran home. I was thrilled to hear those words and to see his bright face.

Of course I wanted to visit him, but it was impossible. I knew it would only make his father angry. I asked two of the teachers to go see him, just so we could know how he was doing. When they went, they learned that he was ill. He had a strange disease on his face. His family took him to the Italian hospital in Damascus.

I was grieved to hear that he was in the hospital and wanted very much to visit him, but I knew that if his father heard, he would be angry. Then one day, I decided that I didn't care what his father might think. I must see the boy. I went to the hospital in Damascus, but he was not there. They had taken him to the American University Hospital in Beirut. The disease had spread all over his face and become quite serious.

After some days, the father brought him back to Damascus. The doctors in Beirut had said, "We have no cure for the boy. He will die. You had better take him back to Syria while he is still alive." They knew that if he died in Lebanon, it would be difficult to get permission from the authorities to move a dead body from Lebanon to Damascus.

His father had taken him back to Damascus in his car. On the way back, the boy had said, "Father, I know I'm going to die. I know I'm going to heaven. I hope you will also give your life to the Lord, so you can also come to heaven. too." The father was so moved. He said, "No son, you're not going to die. I'm taking you back home to Damascus, you see. You are better." But he was not telling the truth.

They arrived in Damascus, and put him in bed. A few hours later the boy again said, "Please Father, I am going to die. I hope you will also give your heart to Jesus!" Then he closed his eyes and that precious son died.

Everybody was crying, brokenhearted. He was only 12 years old, the only son of his father and now he was dead. "No one else will bury my son," the father said, "except that servant of the Lord, the one that my son loved so much. I will ask Rev. Doctorian to do the burial service."

My heart ached, but I was happy to do the burial service. The day of the burial, I took the whole school with me. The boy's body was in a white coffin. The Orthodox school came as well, with the Orthodox priest in front, but I led the procession to the graveyard. Everybody was crying. Everyone was deeply grieved that this young boy, the only son of the tailor, was dead.

At graveyard, I preached, telling the people how this precious son had given his heart to Jesus. "I know that he is not dead," I said. "He is in heaven."

The father broke down, fell on his knees and begged me to pray for him. "I will give my heart to the Lord," he cried, "I want to be saved. I want to go to heaven, so I can see my son one day." All the people were crying as we stood at the gravesite. I prayed for the father. I laid hands on him, and he gave his life to the Lord. We knew the Holy Spirit was moving through the death of that boy, to save his father and the whole family.

To God be the glory!

* * *

Another amazing story from Syria involved a spiritualist. Spiritualists believe that that the spirits of the dead can communicate with the living through a medium. The head spiritualist in Syria was a well-know 54-year-old professor at Damascus University named George Ghathiny. Even the presidents of Syria and Egypt would consult with him, wanting him to go into a trance to ask dead spirits about their future.

While he was practicing his spiritualism, I was having a crusade, a series of tremendous revival meetings in Damascus. We were meeting every day in a Presbyterian church, which was crowded with hundreds coming to the Lord.

One night while I was preaching, I noticed a man in the congregation with white hair. When I gave the invitation for those who wanted to give their lives to the Lord, I saw him stand. I prayed for all the people, then invited them forward. When I opened my eyes, the man with the white hair was gone. Even though he had stood to pray, he had not come forward with the others.

After the meeting I asked some of the brethren if they had noticed him. They said, "Yes, he left just as you were closing in prayer." One of the brothers said, "I recognized him. He is the head spiritualist in Damascus. I wonder why he came to our meetings."

The next morning at eight o'clock, I was at the British School in Damascus where we met each morning to pray. Imagine my surprise when the man with the white hair walked in! He wanted to speak with me, but he could not say a word. His tongue had been supernaturally bound. He had to write down everything to communicate with me.

He wrote that the night before, after he left the meeting, some angels had come and spoken to him. They said his tongue would be bound so that he would not be able to speak, and that he was not to give anyone the messages from the spirits. He had written all of these messages on little pieces of paper.

"What's your name?" I asked him.

"George Ghathiny," he wrote.

"I don't believe it was an angel from the Lord," I said. "I think it must have been a messenger from Satan."

He quickly wrote, "He said he was an angel from the Lord."

"George, I think this angel is a demon in disguise. If a devil has bound your tongue, the Lord can unbind you and loose your tongue. If the Lord has bound your tongue, I can't do a thing."

Everyone present in that prayer meeting was afraid. We all began to pray with one voice, asking Jesus to cover us in His blood.

Then I turned to George and said with authority, "In the name of Jesus, I loose your tongue."

"George, say the name 'Jesus,'" I urged. He tried, but he couldn't. His tongue was still bound.

We all began to pray, "Loose it, Lord! Break this bondage!"

Suddenly George began to shout, "Jesus! Jesus!" His tongue was loosed. The Lord had set him free!

Then I said, "George, I'm coming to your home this afternoon. We need to burn every message from the spirits." He agreed.

Right when I got to George's home, a Muslim man arrived. He was the one who would write down the "prophesies" while George was under the power of the dark spirits. He never came to George's home in the afternoon, so we were not expecting him, but there he was. He saw me. I ignored him and turned to George, "Bring all the papers to me, George."

We went up on the roof of the house. "I am going to burn them," I said.

When the Muslim man heard what we were going to do, he got angry. "You are responsible for this," he insisted.

"Not me, I said, calmly. " Jesus is responsible, but I will burn them."

The Muslim man flew into a rage and left.

I asked for matches and I burned the whole pile of all those devilish papers, those "prophesies" that were supposed to be from the Lord. I knew that every one of them was from an evil spirit. We had a great bonfire up on the roof. I rejoiced and George was so happy to be free from that spiritual darkness. We did it all in the name of Jesus.

· That night, my wife and I were getting into bed. We lived on the second floor. Naomi went to close the door to the balcony and also the inner glass door between the balcony and our room. She had just joined me in bed, when she heard both doors open.

Who had opened the doors? There was no wind or noise. She told me later that she was scared to death. She tried to shake me.

"Samuel," she said, "the doors are open, get up and see what is happening." But I was bound, paralyzed. I could not speak. I could hear my wife saying, "Samuel, Samuel, what's happening?" But I couldn't say a word. Then I saw the devil coming towards me.

Naomi said later that she knew I was alive. My eyes were open and I was breathing, but I did not respond to her questions and she couldn't wake me by shaking.

Suddenly, in my spirit, I shouted, "In the name of Jesus, get out." Instantly Satan was gone and I was loosed. I could speak and move.

"What happened?" my wife asked.

"Naomi, I just saw the devil." We both got on our knees, and prayed together, claiming the blood, covering ourselves with the blood of the Lamb. Then we went to bed and had a wonderful night's rest.

Satan was attacking me, because I had burned those papers.

George was totally free from all Satanic powers. Sometime later he came to Beirut to see me, and I said, "George, how are you?"

Pointing to the Bible in his pocket, he said, "I'm reading it everyday, and I'm living only by the Word of God. I'm rejoicing in the Lord." He had great victory in his life. He was witnessing for Christ, until the day he died and went to be with the Lord.

We knew great victory in the name of Jesus. To God be the glory!

* * *

As the revival started to spread to other parts of Syria, the government of Syria began to be troubled over me. Imagine! Little me! I am not even five foot seven inches tall. The great government of Syria was afraid of me! But it was not me they feared, but the One I represent. His Word is powerful.

The government sent secret police to every meeting. The Holy Ghost showed me who they were and I enjoyed seeing them. When I saw them, I preached better. They gave me inspiration. I got hold of one of them one day and said, "I know you are a secret policeman. I am so glad you are coming, but I have a question for you. I keep seeing different ones every night. Why?"

He said, "To tell you the truth, we've told the Minister of Interior, 'Don't send us to those meetings. There is strange power there. If we keep going, we will become Christians.' So he sends different secret agents every night."

Invitations to preach poured in from all over the Middle East— Jordan, Iraq, Iran, Egypt, Cyprus, and Lebanon. My one-year term in Damascus was drawing to a close, and I felt that I could not stay longer. I asked permission from my church to leave so I could preach the Gospel in other parts of the Middle East. I believed that my God was a great God, and He wanted to shake the Middle East with a mighty Holy Ghost revival.

Then, quite suddenly, the government of Syria put me out of the country. They said I was a "dangerous man." They thought they could stop the revival by getting rid of me. But I told them, "It is too late. The revival fire is already burning."

19

Revival in Egypt

After I was thrown out of Damascus, I went back to Lebanon and then on to Port Said, Egypt. This time, I took Naomi and little Paul with me. The first night, about three hundred precious people gathered in the mission, hungry for the Gospel. The next day we had more. After a week, we had outgrown the church, so we moved outside to a big yard, where we held open-air meetings. By the third week, we had moved to the largest Presbyterian Church in the city, which held several thousand people. During the fourth week, the entire city had heard about the mighty works of God, and every night souls came to the Lord. After a month of meetings in Port Said, we began to receive telegrams and invitations from many parts of Egypt.

We prayed and the Holy Spirit led us to Alexandria. We thought we would stay there a while, so I rented a house for my family. We started preaching in the Presbyterian Church, and then we went from church to church, from place to place, for three months. Thousands heard the Gospel of Christ. I would give the invitation and hundreds of people would come forward with tears in their eyes.

People from all walks of life were finding the Lord as their personal Savior. Invitations continued to pour in from cities and villages all over Egypt. In Cairo, I preached again to the Soul Salvation

Society. Very soon the Spirit of God brought a mighty visitation, and the number grew to a thousand, to two thousand, and soon to four and five thousand people.

For many weeks the Lord sent revival fires into the city of Cairo. The largest churches were opened for the preaching of the Gospel, and the Lord was glorified.

*   *   *

The news of these revivals spread all over the county. A medical doctor in Egypt, Dr. Albert Luka, had a magazine called *Shams el Burr* which means, in Arabic, "The Sun of Righteousness." He put my picture in his magazine with a report of the mighty move of God, and suddenly I began to get invitations to preach. I received over two hundred invitations from all over Egypt. I began to pray, asking God, "Where should I go?" I felt led to go to the city of Asyut, or Assiut as it's called today, then a city of about 200,000, on the Nile, right in the middle of Egypt.

I went by train. When I arrived at the station, I saw a group of about 10 young men in their twenties and thirties, looking for someone, but they did not seem to notice me, so I passed them by.

They had never seen my picture. It is strictly forbidden by the government of Egypt for anyone to print pamphlets or advertise Christian meetings. We could not even use loudspeaker systems in the church building without special permission.

Suddenly one of the young men ran after me and asked in broken English, "Are you Samuel Doctorian?"

"Yes, I am."

He quickly turned and shouted to the others in Arabic, "It's him. He's the evangelist. He's the preacher." They were not expecting someone so young.

They surrounded me, shook my hand, and welcomed me to Asyut. One of them said to the others in Arabic, "Is this Samuel Doctorian? He's just a boy! What can he do?" He did not realize that I understood Arabic and I did not let him know that I knew what he was saying.

Instead I asked in English, "Where are we having the meetings?" They told me that the meetings were to be held in a very big place. They would take me there to see it, but first they wanted to take me to my room.

"No," I said, "I want to see the meeting place. We'll pray there, then I need to go to sleep."

We got into a horse and buggy—they didn't have many cars then—and went through the city of Asyut to the meeting place. They proudly showed me a hall that looked like it could seat about one thousand. I said to them in English, "Brothers, this is too small; we must pray for a bigger place."

The same brother, who had criticized me earlier, said in Arabic, "Let him fill this space first! He wants us to get him a bigger place! Who does he think he is?"

I did not say a word, but I understood everything.

Then I said to them in English, "Let's pray."

I began to pray, "Lord, you're the God of Noah. Just like You brought the animals two by two to the ark, bless this city and bring the people to the meeting, Lord. Fill this place. Let the mighty revival come to the city of Asyut. In Jesus' name, Amen."

I believed that if God wanted to bring the people to the meeting, no one could stop them. God is the One who does the work of revival. It is not the work of man. The Bible says, in Zechariah 4:6, "It is not by might, nor by power, but by My Spirit, says the Lord of Hosts."

After I prayed, they took me to my room. It was a very simple room with a bed, a table, and a chair. The janitor who cleaned the place was wearing a long traditional Arab robe, or *galabiyeh*, which was very dirty. It looked like it was the only one he had and that he never washed it. His hands, face, and clothes were dirty, his hair was not combed, and he had only one eye. This unkempt individual was going to bring my meals—breakfast from one house, lunch from another, and dinner from yet another. I was to eat alone in my room. I tried not to think about all the flies. Egypt has been very "blessed" with flies, especially since the days of Moses. There are more flies than you can imagine. I was sure all those flies would be sampling my food as it traveled the streets of Asyut, but I decided to push this thought from my mind. I would give thanks and eat whatever they brought me.

That night the brothers came and took me to the meeting. To their surprise and my great joy, the hall was packed. After the meeting, I said to some of the brothers, "I think you must start searching for a bigger place." They did not answer. The next night the place was packed and there were three hundred people outside who could not get in. Again God blessed us mightily. I gathered the brothers together and said them, "I am telling you, you must get a bigger place!" The brother who had been so critical earlier, Alfonse Sylvanus, said to them in Arabic, "Don't promise him anything. We don't know why so many are coming. It may just be curiosity. Let's see what happens tomorrow."

Alfonse was the secretary of the group, so they listened to him.

The next night the hall was even more crowded. Many people came early to get seats. It was impossible for everyone to get in. The move of God was so tremendous. I called the brothers and said, "If you don't get a bigger place, I'm going to another city. I have invitations from all over the country."

Alfonse said to them in Arabic, "Whatever he says, let's do it."

"Thank You, Lord," I said to myself. "You answer prayer!"

After the meeting I went to my room. My suitcases and my clothing were gone. I thought, *Somebody has helped himself to my belongings while I was preaching. All stolen!* I called the brothers, "Someone has taken everything from my room!"

They said, "No, no. Don't worry. One of the brothers has taken it to his home. You are going to stay with him."

They took me to the home, and guess whose home it was? It was the home of Alfonse Sylvanus, the same man who had criticized me so many times in Arabic. When he opened the door, he said to me with his head bowed, "Welcome to our humble home."

He said this in English, but I answered him in Arabic.

His head jerked up and his jaw dropped. "You speak Arabic? Have you understood everything I've been saying?"

"Every word."

He turned bright red. "I'm so sorry," he said, lowering his eyes.

"No, Brother Alfonse. Whatever you said was right. It is not Samuel Doctorian, but the God of Samuel that is working in this city. Revival has come to Asyut. To God be the glory!"

20

On Fire in Egypt

More and more people were coming to our nightly meetings. We needed more room. The brothers found a plot of land that would seat four thousand people. The land belonged to a goldsmith. After the brothers got more chairs, we began meeting there. News of the revival spread all over the city of Asyut.

The next night we filled the new meeting place. The revival was so tremendous that I could not leave Asyut. I stayed a second week. Every night hundreds and hundreds came to Christ.

I would tell them the Scripture, "That whoever calls on the name of the LORD shall be saved" (Joel 2:32 NKJV). "Call on the name of the Lord," I would urge the crowd, and then someone would call out, "Lord, save me!" Then the crowd would say, "Amen." Another one would say, "Lord, have mercy on me!" and the crowd would shout, "Amen!" Many were crying out and giving their lives to the Lord.

The third week there was even greater revival. The revival was so strong that people stopped going to coffee bars and cinemas—they were all coming to the meetings. Hundreds were saved every night.

God gave me faith to buy the piece of land where we were holding our open-air meeting. God told me to raise the money from the people in Asyut. When I told the brothers my plan, they said, "Brother Samuel, you don't know these Egyptians. The people in Asyut have a reputation for being very stingy." But I believed God.

One night the brethren were taking the offering. A woman put a heavy bag in the offering plate. The bag was so heavy that the usher at the end of that row nearly lost his balance when they passed the plate to him.

When the meeting was over the brothers called me, "Brother Samuel, something terrible has happened."

"What?" I asked.

"A woman has put all her gold in the offering plate."

"Hallelujah!" I said.

"Don't say that," they scolded. "If her husband finds out he could make trouble!"

The next day, three of the brothers went with me to her home. We brought all the gold—18 pieces—in a bag. The husband and wife were both there. We asked to speak to the husband privately. When we were alone, we told him, "We have something very important to discuss with you. Last night, your wife was in our meeting. She put all of this gold in the offering. We brought it back to you."

He began to cry. "Never," he said. "I will never take it back. A few days ago, I saw the change in my wife. Last night I was in the meeting and I got saved. Hallelujah! If we had more gold, we would give it all. Our home has become like heaven."

God had provided. In a short time we had all the money we needed to buy the land.

* * *

The whole time I was in Asyut, Naomi and my son, Paul, who was not quite two, had been living in Alexandria, four hundred miles to the north. I had not thought I would be in Asyut so long, but the brothers did not want me to go. Now that my living conditions were better, they offered to bring my precious wife and son to me. Some friends of ours, Armenians in Alexandria, put Naomi and Paul on the train for Asyut and I met them at the station. I was so happy to see them.

Now that I was living with Alfonse, and my wife and son were with me, my life was much better. I was no longer eating alone. Every day we would be invited to a brother's house for lunch or dinner, and 10 of the brothers would join me around the table.

Then trouble came. I began to receive threats. Mobs said they were going to kill me. One night the brothers came to me trembling. "Brother Samuel," they said, "we have terrible news. We must stop the meetings."

"Why?"

"The governor of Asyut has ordered us to stop."

"Which governor?" I asked. "The one down here, or the One up in heaven?"

"The one down here."

"The One up in heaven is telling me to continue. I will not listen to anyone down here who tells me to stop." I was not just being stubborn. I had a strong conviction from God that I should not be afraid. So I refused to listen to them.

"Brother Samuel," they said, "they will kill you!"

I said, "They killed my grandparents. They killed my aunts and uncles. They killed my loved ones. All my relatives were massacred for Jesus' sake. They can kill me, too. I won't stop the meetings."

Three brothers went to the governor to beg, "Please let us continue."

The governor got so angry he threw them out and told them, "Tonight, I am sending my soldiers. If he stands up and preaches, I will order them to shoot him on the platform."

The brothers came to me, "We must stop the meeting. We can't continue."

I said, "I am not going to stop."

"Brother Samuel, the soldiers will shoot you."

"I don't care," I said. "I am going to preach."

Usually, we had 10 or 12 of the leading brothers on the platform, but that night no one would sit up there with me. Everyone sat in the audience. They were afraid but I refused to be cowed.

That night I preached to a great crowd. The loudspeaker boomed out over a sea of faces. Thousands of people were there. My wife, Naomi, was seated with little Paul on her lap on a balcony of an apartment building overlooking the open space where we were holding our meetings. All the balconies were crowded, and there were crowds of people on the rooftops of nearby buildings.

Suddenly, I saw 12 soldiers armed with British automatic tommy guns elbowing their way through the crowd. I watched as they worked their way closer. When they were about 50 feet from the platform, they raised their guns and took aim. I faltered. My words came out a jumble. I didn't know what I was saying. The color drained from my face. Those seated in the front turned to see what had shaken me.

I looked at the soldiers and said, "You can shoot me, but before you do, I want to tell you three things. First, when you touch a child of God, you are touching the apple of His eye. Second, when you persecute me, you persecute my Jesus. And third, when you shoot me, God will raise up, right from this congregation, hundreds of young men who will set Egypt on fire for God!"

I was thinking of how the very man who ordered the stoning of Stephen later became Paul, the man who spread the Gospel throughout the Roman world. I could hear women in the congregation crying. I looked up at Naomi and Paul. I saw that Naomi's head was bowed, and she was weeping. I bowed my head, waiting for the bullets to come.

Then suddenly such power filled the place! Although I speak four languages, there is no language, no words to describe what I felt right then. New power came on me. I opened my eyes to see why they were not shooting. Every head was bowed, every gun was lowered. I said, "Thank you, soldiers." Then I preached another 15 minutes.

That night hundreds came forward to give their hearts to the Lord! We counted only the men—three hundred men came forward, as well as hundreds of women. I prayed with all of them. Some of those who came forward that night are preachers and evangelists in the land of Egypt today.

The next day, the governor was thrown out of office on order from the authorities in Cairo, and a new governor was appointed. The new governor gave us permanent permission to meet there. He changed the name of the street near our meeting place to *Revival Street* or "Shargh Inteeghash" in Arabic. To God be the glory.

We built a building on that site that seats two thousand people. The church that meets there is part of the Soul Salvation Society, an independent evangelical church under the umbrella of the Presbyterian Church.

Many years later in 1987, I preached to a crowd of ten thousand in that building. We were celebrating the 77th anniversary of Lillian Trasher's orphanage. Lillian was a great American missionary who took care of thousands of Egyptian orphans. She's in heaven now, but while she was in Asyut, we were dear friends. That glorious day, I was preaching and who was sitting in the front row but the new governor himself! Glory to God!

Of all the places that I have gone, we had the greatest revival, in numbers and in power, in the city of Asyut. Every time I have gone back, that meeting place is crowded. Thousand have turned to the Lord and the whole city has been shaken by the power of God.

*   *   *

That was not the only time my life was threatened in Egypt.

Once, on the train, a man tried to take my life. We had been holding revival meetings in Sohag. When I left, five hundred people came to the station to say good-bye. It was not easy to say goodbye because each one wanted to kiss my cheek in farewell. Colonel Kamal Wilson, a colonel in the Egyptian tourist police was traveling with me, to protect me, along with my father, and a Syrian singer who sang at my meetings.

We were sitting in the lounge having a cup of tea, when a wild looking man rushed straight at me and said, "I have to speak to you."

The colonel jumped up between the man and me but the man knocked him to the floor. I grabbed hold of the man and said, "Just a minute. You don't have to be so rough. What is it you want?"

He insisted on speaking to me privately.

"Okay," I said. "I will come. Which compartment are you in?"

He gave me the number and left.

My three travel companions told me that I should not go. "He looks wild!" they said.

"I don't care. I think he is wounded. I am going to see him."

I went back through the train looking for the compartment number he had given me. I found him sitting in his compartment alone. Back then, the trains in Egypt and much of Europe were divided into small compartments of six to eight seats arranged in two rows facing each other, like a little room.

He was holding his head in his hands.

I sat opposite him. I could hear him mumbling, "My sins, my sins!"

He was troubled.

"Can I help you?" I asked, gently.

"How can you help me?" he shouted, angrily. "You don't know what I have done! I have killed three men. I have committed every sin you can imagine. Last night I was drunk," he continued. "I saw a crowd outside a church. I pushed my way in. There was nowhere to sit so I stood in the aisle. You were preaching. You named every sin I've done. I got so angry with you. I heard them announce when and where you were leaving.

"I went home. I couldn't sleep all night. I decided to get on the same train as you, so I could kill you." At this, he pulled a gun from his pocket and pointed it at me. He had his finger on the trigger. He was right across from me, just three feet away. My first thought was that I could wrest the gun from him. But then I felt the presence of God giving me peace.

I said to him, "You could shoot me. You could kill me. But what would happen to you?"

His hand began to shake. He put the gun back in his pocket.

I took a deep breath.

He began to cry. In 15 minutes we were on our knees together in that train compartment, weeping as he gave his heart to Jesus. When we finished, I got up to open the door of the compartment, and there were the three brothers—my father, the colonel, the singer—standing outside the door with tears in the their eyes.

I said, "Come in! Greet our new brother in the Lord!"

The next day I was preaching to the Soul Salvation Society in Cairo. There were five thousand people at the meeting. I was telling the story of what happened on the train. Of course, I did not tell the audience that the man had murdered three men. I only said that he was on the train and had decided to kill me.

Suddenly I heard someone shouting from the back, "Brother Samuel, I'm here!" He was in the meeting! Afterwards he came up to me and hugged me. He looked totally changed. He was clean, shaved, and well dressed. I will never forget what he said with tears in his eyes, "I am going back to my city, a new husband to my wife, a new father to my children."

21

Secret Police

We had wonderful times of revival in Egypt. I preached to many different denominations: the Evangelical Church, the Holiness Church, the Baptist Church, the Brethren Church, the Presbyterian Church—wherever God would open the door. One time I brought my old friend from seminary, John Crouch, to Beirut and Egypt. When John saw the thousands of people and the work of God in the Middle East, he said to me, "Samuel, do you remember how we believed God for this back when we were students?"

It was a wonderful time, but the more the fire spread, the more we were persecuted. One time I was in Aswan in Upper Egypt where the Egyptians built the world's largest dam on the river Nile. It took them eight years—from 1960 to 1968—to build that dam. Three hundred engineers worked on the dam. One of them happened to be a Christian brother, who at the time, was 36 and single. He was a faithful and dear friend who loved me very much. One day he invited me to his apartment for dinner. He lived in a one-story government apartment building, in an area populated by hundreds of government apartments set in rows side-by-side. Inside he had one bedroom, a kitchen, living room, and dining room. He was cooking the meal, while I sat on the sofa reading an Arabic newspaper. Suddenly, the doorbell rang. I got up to answer the door.

As I was opening the door, the Holy Spirit warned me, "Be careful! He is a secret police agent and he is after you." I looked at the man standing before me. He was wearing western clothes, a suit and tie and was quite well dressed.

"Welcome, dear man!" I said. "I have never met one of the secret police before."

He looked shocked. He asked, "Do you know me?"

"No," I said, "I have never seen you before, but come in."

He came in and he sat down on a chair.

Suddenly the Holy Spirit began to tell me this man's secrets. Something this man was doing that he had hidden from everyone.

I told him. The Spirit told me more details.

I repeated them to the spy.

"Just a minute," he said. "How can you know these things? Who told you about me?"

I smiled at him and leaned forward. "A wonderful Person," I said. "One Who is here right now with us. He is telling me all about you."

He looked around and said, "There is nobody here!" He looked behind him through the open kitchen door where my young host was cooking dinner.

I caught a glimpse of my host. He looked pale and shaken. I turned back to our guest. "A wonderful Person is telling me about you right now. He is telling me top secret information about you."

The Holy Ghost gave me even more details, which I repeated to the man.

The man began to shake, trembling from head to foot. "Just a minute," he said in a tight voice. "Don't say any more. Who is telling you about me?"

"Who is it?" I repeated. "It is the Third Person of the Trinity, the Holy Spirit."

"Ah," he said. "I've heard that you Christians believe that God the Father has a Son, but who is this Third One?"

"Without the Third One," I said, "we would have no Bible. Without the Third One, we would have no birth of Christ. Without the Third One, we would have no resurrection." I began to talk to him about the Holy Ghost. The more I talked, the more troubled he looked.

Suddenly he sprang to his feet and said, "I have to go! I have to go!"

"Okay," I said. "You can go—but He is coming after you!"

The man was trembling. He reached for the door and raced down the steps. Halfway down he turned to see who was coming after him.

After he left, my young host came into the room. In a quavering voice, he said, "Do you know who that was? He is the most dangerous man in all of Upper Egypt. He goes after Christians. He can throw you out of the country, Brother Samuel. I should not have left you alone with him, but I was so afraid. I was afraid that I might say the wrong thing and get us both in trouble."

I looked at him calmly. "I am hungry, my dear boy," I said. "Where's the chicken?"

He looked startled.

"Don't worry." I reassured him. "The Lord will take care of him."

After we ate, I went to the railway station to meet some friends who were coming in from Cairo, six hundred miles away. The train was late. I was standing on the crowded train platform when suddenly somebody grabbed my upper arm in an iron grip. I thought, *Who is pulling so hard?* I turned and saw the same secret police agent that I had spoken to earlier that evening. My first thought was that I was in trouble, but then I looked into his eyes and saw that his eyes were moist. *Ah,* I thought, *I am not in trouble, this spy is the one who's in trouble!*

He escorted me to one side of the railway station. When we were alone he said, through his tears, "Everything you said about me is true. I want to become a Christian. Can I become a secret disciple to Jesus?" he asked. "You know, if I become Christian, I will lose my job. I will have to leave the country. They will kill me."

My first thought was that no one can be a secret disciple of Jesus for long. If you belong to Christ you cannot deny Him. You are open to anyone. You don't hide it. You are not ashamed of it. You let others be ashamed. You can't be ashamed of Jesus.

But I knew that the Holy Spirit would show him that. He wanted to accept Christ, so I prayed with him. I led him to Christ.

Tears flowed down his cheeks. When we were done praying, he gave me the warmest hug.

I thought, *He came to catch me, but he was caught by the mighty Holy Ghost!*

* * *

After I left Aswan, I went to Luxor, a historic city famous for the Great Pyramids. When the chief of police there heard that I was in the city, he called me and said, "I must see you!"

Lord, I thought, *am I in trouble now?* I went to the chief of police. He welcomed me into his office, closed the door, and then pulled two chairs out so we could sit opposite each other.

"What have you done to my friend?" he asked.

"Who is your friend?" I asked.

He gave me the name of the secret police agent in Aswan.

I said, "I have done nothing to him."

"Whatever has happened to him," he said, "I want to happen to me."

We fell down on our knees, together, that chief of police and I, and he gave his life to Jesus. That is the work of the mighty Holy Spirit of God!

22

The Woman on Death Row

One of the precious souls who was saved during my time in Asyut was the chief warden of the second largest prison in Egypt. Before he got saved he had been a nominal Christian. He was in charge of 1,600 prisoners, and every night he brought a small group of them to the meetings. Several notorious prisoners got saved, and then the chief warden himself got saved!

One day he invited me to his home at the prison compound to play tennis, eat dinner and relax. After we played tennis, we were visiting in his office when he asked me if I would like to see the gallows where they hang the criminals.

I was curious, so after we finished our coffee he took me to the place. It was a terrible sight. I saw the rope. I saw the piece of wood, which covered the opening in the floor, on which the criminal stands. I saw how they kick the wood away so that the condemned one hangs in the air. It was a moving experience.

I said to him, "Tell me exactly what you do when you hang someone." He showed where he stands and where the condemned one stands facing him. He explained how he pronounces the final judgment from the court, how a guard puts a sack over the head of the guilty one, and how a guard leads him to the gallows, puts the rope round his neck and hangs him.

I asked the chief warden, "Will you stand in your usual spot?"

He stood there, and I went and stood at the place of the condemned. "Now pronounce judgment on me," I said.

He was shocked. "No. I can't. You don't really want me to do that!"

"I just want to hear it. Go ahead and say the words. Say the words that you say when you hang the condemned one. Just do it."

He was the commander over a 1,600 prisoners, but he was my spiritual son, so he did what I asked.

As soon as he said the words, I shouted, "Now there is no more condemnation for those who are in Christ Jesus. I am free!"

Gratitude washed over me for the glorious freedom we have in Christ. We shall not die but live forever because Jesus died for us. When you are a true Christian, there is nothing more miraculous than that!

I asked the warden, "Are there any prisoners that will hang soon?"

"Yes, there are two women who will be hung soon. I am just waiting for the final order from Cairo."

"You hang women, also?" I asked.

"Yes, though we haven't done it for a long time."

"What have these women done?"

He told me their dreadful crimes.

"Can I see them?" I asked. He took me to the women's section of the prison. I opened the little window in the door and looked in. The woman inside looked angry and twisted, like a witch. The warden said she was 54 years old and had killed her husband with an axe while he was sleeping in the field, because he had married another woman.

I looked in the next cell. This woman was much younger, only 23. The instant she saw me looking at her, she cried out, "Help me! Help me!" I couldn't bear to look. Tears filled my eyes. I closed the little window and turned away. "What has she done?" I asked.

"It is awful! She killed a 12-year-old girl, and stole her earrings, to get opium and hashish for her husband."

"She's married?" I asked.

"Yes. She's married and has three children."

My heart ached. I couldn't bear to hear anymore.

We went back to the warden's home, but I could not get that young woman's face out of my mind.

Later, one of the prison guards drove me back to the house where I was staying in Asyut. I was going to take an afternoon nap before the evening meeting. As is my custom, I fell on my knees to pray. In my mind I saw that young woman's face and heard her plea, "Help me!"

I began to pray, "Lord, is there anything I can do?"

Suddenly my room was filled with the presence of the Lord. An angel of the Lord stood in front of me. He opened a scroll and read: "That young mother is not the murderer. She did not kill that girl. Her husband killed the girl. He told her that she should take the blame and confess because the government would not punish a woman as severely as a man. He told her that she would be out of prison in a few years. He said that if she would not confess, that he would kill her and their three children. So she confessed with fear and trembling. She said she was the murderer."

I was shaken to the depths of my soul. I called the chief warden and said, "Come quickly, I must speak with you."

"What is it?"

"I cannot talk about it on the phone. This is extremely important. Please come."

"I will be right there."

When he got there, I closed the door to the room and made him sit down. Then I told him everything. He was shaken and bewildered.

"A real angel? A heavenly angel?"

"Yes. A real angel. Just now."

"I don't know what to do," he said. "It is not in my hands. The case is closed. She has been condemned. Any minute the order to hang her will come from the court in Cairo. I must hang this woman."

"You dare not! She is not the murderer! Her husband is the murderer!"

"What do you want me to do?"

"Go back to the prison. She is going to confess. When she tells you, word for word, what the angel told me, you will know that what I am saying is true."

"Okay. I will go back, but I have never had anything like this happen before in all my life."

As soon as he got to the prison one of the officers told him that a woman on death row wanted to talk with him.

"Which one?"

"The young one."

"Bring her in." Then he had another officer hide a tape player in the room.

The young mother came to the office trembling, a little bit ashamed because she had only a sack over her body. She asked if she could speak to the warden alone. He agreed. They closed the door but the tape player recorded it all. She confessed with tears, word by word, exactly what the Lord had told me.

The warden sent the tapes to Cairo. The judge declared a mistrial. The real murderer was caught, judged, and hung. The authorities secretly moved the young mother and her children to another village so the husband's relatives could not take revenge. They are still alive today.

The whole story was printed in the *Al-Ahram* newspaper in Egypt, but I asked them not to use my name because I knew the murderer's relatives would kill me if they knew my part in bringing him to justice. God knew. He is just. He will not forsake us. Praise His name.

22

America

The first time I went to America was in April 1955. I was 25 years old. For nine years, since I was 16, I had been praying, "Oh Lord, take me to America one day!" Even as a teenager, growing up in Jerusalem, I had heard so much about America from our pastor, who had graduated from Pasadena Nazarene College, and from American missionaries. I thought that if I could only get to America, I would be in paradise. While I was still a teenager, the Lord witnessed in my spirit that He would bring me to America one day.

Now the moment had arrived. I flew from Cairo to New York. The second the plane touched down at Kennedy Airport, I unfastened my seatbelt and fell on my knees in the airplane. I knew that I shouldn't take the seatbelt off before the plane had taxied to the gate, but I couldn't wait. Right there in the plane, I prayed, "Oh God, use me in this country."

I spent one night in the YMCA in New York, then took the train to Chicago. I had been invited to attend the convention of the National Association of Evangelicals. I was one of 12 speakers from all over the world. I was to represent the Middle East. Each of us had five minutes to speak. When my turn came, I spoke on the mighty move of God in Syria, Lebanon, Egypt and Jordan. I stopped after only four and a half minutes and sat down. They all clapped. They wanted me to continue, but I felt I had said what I had to say.

After the meeting, over 20 preachers, from all over America, invited me to come to their churches. One asked where I was staying and when he heard I was in a hotel, he said, "Come and stay in my home. Two presidents of mission societies are staying with me, too, and I want you to meet them."

That was how God opened the door to my ministry in America.

I remember that at that convention, someone asked me if I would like a hot dog. I had been hungry just a moment before, but at the word "hot dog" my appetite vanished. I thought that Americans ate dogs! I didn't eat any hot dogs on that trip, but I later learned that they are quite tasty.

*   *   *

The next time I went to America, I took my wife and our little son, Paul. It was December 29, 1955, and we set out from Beirut for the United States on a DC-7 plane. Back then a DC-7 was a modern jet plane with low wings and two prop engines on each side. But it had a limited range and so we were scheduled to fly to Rome, then Brussels, then Shannon, and then New York. As we flew on the first leg of the journey, over Turkey, Greece and Italy, 24,000 feet in the air, I thought about the Apostle Paul. How long had it taken him to travel from Beirut to Rome? Here we were, flying to Rome in just six hours!

We stopped in Rome for about an hour, and then boarded the plane again to continue on to Brussels. The plane climbed higher and higher to 20,000 feet where it leveled off for the short trip. Looking out the window, I saw the beautiful coastline of Italy against the deep blue water of the Mediterranean Sea.

By 9:30 P.M. we were getting sleepy. The pilot announced that we would be in Belgium in three and a half hours. My wife, Naomi, soon fell asleep. I was holding Paul, when suddenly a loud siren went off. At first I thought, *The Lord is coming!* But then an explosion rocked the plane. I looked out. Just outside the right window, one of the engines was on fire. All around me, people grew pale and reached for their seat belts. I was scared, and I was not the only one—everyone was crying out to God for help. My wife and I began to cry. Up ahead I could see the mountains of southern France. I wondered, *Where will we fall—in the mountains or in the sea? Or will we even survive long enough to fall?* Soon the flames would reach the fuel tanks causing an explosion that would tear the plane to pieces and bring death to us all.

There was nothing that we could do but wait to die. We were trapped. On a boat, there is always the possibility of getting away in a life raft. In a car accident, there is always the possibility that help is on the way, but in an airplane there was nothing we could do but wait for the end to come.

Behind me, two women were praying to Mary, crying out, "Oh Mary, Mother of Jesus, please tell Jesus! Please help us!" I was so glad that I did not need to go to Mary, that I could go to my Redeemer Jesus, Himself. Glory to God!

I started praying and suddenly a spirit of praise came on me. I began to thank God. I thanked Him that the three of us—my wife, my son and myself—were ready to die. Before the burning plane reached the ground, we would be with the Lord. I thanked Him I had done my utmost for Him the night before. I had preached to a large meeting in Beirut. Many had listened to the message and turned to God. I was the last one to leave the church. I had stayed to pray with each one; I had done my utmost. I was also thankful that our little family would die together. My son would not be an orphan; my wife would not be a widow. We would close our eyes down here, and open them in the presence of the Lord.

All around me, people were closing the curtains so they would not have to see the growing flames. Any second we expected to hear the explosion that would end our lives.

As I was praising God, suddenly faith came into my heart. Why was I afraid? God was not finished with me yet. There was still so much to be done. My God was mighty. Looking out the window of the plane, I could see no cause for hope, but looking through the window of faith, I began to be filled with a great hope and began to lift up my heart to God in prayer. I sensed that God was going to save us through a great miracle.

I got up from my seat and went to the front of the plane, near the front door, so I could be alone with the Lord and pray. I began to lift my voice up to heaven and weep. "Lord, surely You do not want me to die now. You are a great God. You do great miracles. Show Your power today. Remember Your promises to me. All that You have said You would do through my unworthy life. Lord," I cried, "Surely, You do not want me to die now!"

I began to cry harder, not because I was afraid—the fear was gone—but the fear had been replaced by a tremendous burden. "Lord," I cried, "enemies have tried to kill me in the Middle East. Your enemies hate me. If I die now, my enemies will rejoice. When they hear that I have burned to death in the air, they will be very glad. Lord, the devil wants to hinder Your work, but I am glad that You can override the power of the devil. Oh God, You are the God of Shadrach, Meshach and Abednego. Just as You delivered them from the fiery furnace, deliver me!"

As I was praying, I felt a hand grip my shoulder. At first, I thought it was the stewardess telling me to get back to my seat. I looked around but no one was there. But I could still feel the hand. Then I heard a voice saying, "Samuel, I shall save you and save everyone in this airplane. I shall deliver you."

"Hallelujah," I cried, thanking the Lord from the depths of my heart. "Lord," I said, "Satan may be the prince of the air, but You are the Lord of the universe and nothing is too difficult for You. I know that all things are possible to him that believes. Thank You, Lord."

I went back to my seat bubbling with joy. When I looked out the window the fire was even larger, yet I felt in my heart even more assurance than before. "Naomi," I said to my wife, "The Lord Jesus just spoke to me and told me that nothing is going to happen and we are going to be saved."

"I see," she said. I was thankful that she believed me. I felt full of confidence.

We looked out the window again. We were seated on the left side of the plane, and the fire was on the right side, but we could see the dancing flames from our seats. By now the fire had completely engulfed the engine. Even as the fire grew, we were confident that God had spoken, and we were certain that His Word is true. He is the omnipotent Lord. He never changes and He never lies.

With great excitement, I stood and shouted, "Don't be afraid. The Lord told me that we will be delivered. Watch and you shall see the mighty hand of God rescue us."

A Turkish doctor who was sitting next to us said, "But look, the fire is growing!"

"I am not looking through that window," I insisted. "I am looking through the window of faith. You shall see the mighty hand of God deliver us."

I was encouraging people, rejoicing in God's promise, when suddenly, the entire engine vanished. The co-pilot and the navigator rushed back through the cabin and peered out the windows over the wing. They got a flashlight and looked some more, but the flaming engine had dropped off the plane. They seemed dumbfounded. They could not understand what had happened, but I explained that the mighty hand of God had touched the engine and made it fall from the plane.

Soon we heard the pilot say over the intercom, "The plane is under control. Do not be afraid; we will be all right. We are returning to Rome. Keep your seat belts fastened until the end of the journey."

When we reached Rome, a huge crowd of firemen, policemen, and reporters met us—all waiting to see if the plane would land safely or catch fire again.

We emerged from the plane with inexpressible joy in our hearts and tears on our faces. What a tremendous experience! What a miracle! Our hearts cried out, *Glory be to the name of Jesus!*

After we landed in Rome, some of the passengers came to me and said, "We were so glad, Brother Doctorian, that you were with us in that plane. We felt our lives were saved because you were there."

"Do not thank me," I replied. "Give the glory to Jesus for He is the same Lord, yesterday, today and forever."

Understandably, most of the passengers, did not want to continue their travels. Naomi, Paul and I were the only ones, by the grace of God, who transferred to the next available flight, and with God's mighty protection, were able to reach New York, our final destination.

The dear brother who picked us up at the airport had a copy of the *Chicago Tribune* tucked under his arm. He showed us the front page. "Samuel, did you hear that an airplane was in the air and the engine exploded and caught fire, but the passengers miraculously survived!"

"We were on that very plane," I told him. The newspaper article described how the engine had hit the ground on the shore of Italy where it continued to burn for nearly three hours.

I was so thankful. Just as God spoke to the Apostle Paul when his ship was in great danger, telling him to not be afraid because every life would be spared, so God had spoken to me in that fiery plane and delivered our lives.

I praise God that He is a God of miracles Who is able to do exceedingly more than we could ask or imagine. He is the God Who delivered Daniel from the lion's den. He is the God Who delivered Shadrach, Meschach and Abednego from the fiery furnace. He is the God Who met Elijah's every need. He is the God Who has done great miracles in every generation of the human race. He will do the same for you if you put your trust in Him.

* * *

On my third trip to America, in 1956, I spoke first at an Armenian church in New Jersey. Afterwards, I decided to fly to Washington, D.C., because the Mennonites there had invited me to speak at several of their churches. After the meeting in New Jersey, the pastor of that church drove me to the airport, but once we got there he could not find a parking place. I told him, "You don't need to come inside. Just drop me off. God bless you."

I went inside and handed my ticket to the ticket agent. I needed to change my ticket so I could fly to Washington, D.C. The agent checked it, then told me it would cost 20 dollars to change my ticket.

"I only have ten!" I told her. I did not tell her that those 10 dollars were supposed to pay for my hotel room that night. In those days, a motel was six dollars. I was trying to decide what to do, when the pastor ran up to the counter. He had found a parking place and was hoping to catch me before I left. He said goodbye, hugged me, and then he said, "I forgot to give you this envelope."

There was 10 dollars inside. I turned back to the counter and gave the agent 20 dollars for my ticket change. Now I had my ticket, but I did not know where I would stay in Washington, D.C. The Mennonites were not picking me up until the next day, and now I had nothing to pay for a hotel room.

On the plane I was seated next to a tall fellow who kept asking me questions. "Father what are you doing here? Where are you from?" One question after another. I felt like I was being interrogated. *Lord*, I asked, *will he never stop?* The flight from New Jersey to Washington was only one hour, but it seemed much longer. Just as we were landing, he opened his wallet and handed me 10 dollars. "Here," he said, "Father, this may help you."

When I think back on this, I smile. Who gives away money on an airplane? I had never heard of such a thing, but God knew my need and He did not fail me.

When I got to Washington, D.C., I checked into my hotel. The next day the Mennonites came and took me to their church, and we had a wonderful time.

24

$\mathcal{B}eirut$

After we left Egypt, the Lord brought me back to Beirut in 1956 with a heavy burden on my heart for revival in this key city. For weeks, I prayed and fasted. I begged ministers and pastors to come together so we could have united meetings where the Holy Spirit could work in our hearts. After persevering and praying by faith, the Lord began to do wonders in the city of Beirut.

The first wonder was that so many different denominations agreed to meet together. We started meeting in the largest Armenian Evangelical Church in Beirut. Then we went to another Armenian Evangelical Church and then to another district, from church to church as the Spirit of the Lord began to move. Hundreds of lost souls came to the Lord Jesus and hundreds of believers were revived with a visitation of the Holy Spirit.

At first we met in the churches, but then God miraculously gave us a huge tent that seated three thousand. I say miraculously because the way we got that tent was a miracle. The year before, while I was preaching in Alexandria, Egypt, I had seen a vision of a great tent. I had been praying about the lack of space. So many people were coming to our meetings in Egypt that we couldn't find a place big enough to hold the crowd. We were using the auditorium of the American College in Alexandria, which seated about 1500, but it was too small.

"Lord," I prayed, "everywhere You are taking me is touched by revival, but we don't have room for all the people. We are working in difficult lands, countries controlled by Muslims who won't let us use football fields or stadiums for our meetings. What should we do?"

Immediately a picture of a gigantic white tent popped into my mind. I had never seen a tent like that before. I did not know that there were such tents. This was before I gone to the West, so I didn't know about the great tent meetings they have in America. In my mind, I simply saw a huge tent. I was thrilled to think that there were such tents. I wondered, *Where can I get one?* I searched, but there was nothing like that in the Middle East.

Shortly after I got the vision, I made my first trip to North America. I was in Kitchener, Ontario, in Canada, looking at a newspaper when I saw a photo of an enormous tent. My eyes nearly popped out. It was the same kind of tent I had seen in my vision.

I showed the picture to some brothers and asked, "Where is this place?"

"About 20 miles away."

"Take me there!" I said.

A group of Mennonite brothers were putting up the tent. One of them was a preacher named Myron Augsburger. Myron was 25 years old, just like me. We shook hands. In the Middle East we hug and kiss each other's cheeks, but Mennonites shake hands. From the moment our hands clasped, I felt our hearts knit together.

The next Sunday morning, I was going to preach at Dr. Oswald Smith's church in Toronto. Myron said he had heard about that dear brother and asked if he could join me. His tent services weren't going to start until the evening. So Myron rode to Toronto with us. You could feel our friendship grow as we traveled along.

I wanted to ask him about the tent. Someone had told me that a tent like that could cost about ten thousand dollars. But another person had said, "Samuel you will never get one! They cost at least $20,000." I wanted to know. "Myron," I said, "before I came to America, I had a vision of a huge tent like yours. I would like to get one for our meetings in the Middle East. You have one, so you must know. How much are they?"

He looked at me. "At least $50,000."

"Lord!" I gasped. "$50,000! Five, zero, zero, zero, zero!"

When I got back to Kitchener, I told the congregation about my dream of having a tent for our meetings in the Middle East. That evening, I received an envelope. Inside, a 17-year-old girl had placed five dollars with a letter that said: "I was supposed to go tonight to a youth banquet. It would have cost me five dollars. I am going to sacrifice going to that banquet. I want to give my five dollars for the tent."

I wept when I read the letter. I fell on my knees in the cabin where I was staying and put the letter and the five dollars before the Lord. "Lord," I said, "I've got the five. You add the zeros."

I will never forget how the Lord supplied everything that we needed. In a few short months we had everything—not only the tent, but two thousand chairs, a generator, a Hammond Organ and a loudspeaker system. The equipment and tents filled four trucks. We shipped everything to Beirut.

I was eagerly awaiting the arrival, but when the shipment got to Beirut, I could not get the customs officials to release the equipment. Lebanon used to be under the French, and they have a strange system that requires the approval of many different offices. I went from office to office. I visited 18 offices in that customs building and everyone said, "No, No, No." No one would help me.

I began to pray and fast. God confirmed the vision. All the equipment was in the port. Now God had to get it out of customs. I continued to fast and pray, and believe God for a miracle.

Then one day I heard that my file was on the customs director's desk. I prayed, and then went to see him.

The guard out front would not let me in. "He is too busy to see you," he insisted.

I am glad the Lord has given me strong voice. I spoke up, hoping the director would hear me. "I NEED TO SEE THE DIRECTOR. I AM THE MAN WITH THE TENT AND ALL THE EQUIPMENT."

The guard would not let me through. I continued to explain my mission in a loud clear voice.

The director opened the door. "What's going on out here?" he asked.

"I want to see you, but he won't let me," I answered softly, motioning to the guard.

"Come in, Father, come in," he said, waving me in.

I came in.

"What can I do for you?" he asked.

I told the director about my vision and God's provision. "The equipment is here," I said, "if I can only get it through customs."

"Oh," he said, placing his finger on a thick folder. Are you the man who has all this equipment?"

I nodded, then thought to myself, *I am so small and the equipment is so big. But God is the God of David. It only took one stone to hit Goliath and knock him down. He is the same God today. Hallelujah!*

The director looked at me and said, "You know, I am a Christian, too." He was Greek Orthodox! "If it was for a church, I would help you, but I have never heard of a church that goes from place to place."

"You don't understand what the church is," I said.

"But I am a Christian!"

"The church is not the building, Sir."

"It's not the building?"

"The church is you, it's me. It is the people of God. This tent is for the church."

"Oh, I see."

Thank God, he saw!

"All right," he said. "You can go now. I will clear everything. I'll sign the release and you will be able to get your equipment soon."

"Director," I said. "Thank you for your help. I have spent a month in this building going from office to office, trying to convince people to say, 'Yes.' Now my request will have to go to back to every office with your directive saying that you have approved it. It is going to take another month. Can't you give me the papers and let me walk them through? I know every office. I know every person in the building. Let me take it myself."

"That is not the way we do things," he said. Then he looked at me and said, "All right." He signed the document and gave it to me.

I rushed into the next office. When the man saw me, he shook his head, and said to his co-workers, "He's back again."

"Yes, I'm back," I said, smiling. "The director said 'yes.' Please sign here."

I went to the next office. I had the greatest time—everyone—Muslims, Maronites, Christians—they all had to sign, "Yes, yes, yes." By the end of the day all of the equipment was cleared from customs, without paying one penny in duty. God is a great God. Hallelujah!

As soon as we got the tent, we set it up in Beirut and moved in. It seated three thousand people. We held meetings for the Armenian people, every day for 16 weeks. The whole city was talking about Jesus.

Then the Arab churches got together and asked me to preach to them also. So a few months later, I started preaching in the Arab churches. The Lord blessed us. Those revival services went on for 10 weeks, every night.

Many hundreds of Arabs were gloriously converted by the power of God. Nominal Christians—Orthodox, Maronite, and Protestant—also surrendered their life to God and are living for the Lord today.

Glory to the Name of the Lord!

* * *

It was a wonderful but exhausting time. During those weeks of tent meetings, my darling daughter, Jasmine, was born on August 28, 1956.

I was young and healthy, just 26 years old, but I would get so tired. Night after night I stayed late to pray for people. I was always the last one to leave the tent, after leading hundreds to the Lord, my heart burning with the fire of the Holy Ghost. There was no time to rest. I got worn out. During the day people would drop by to see me, and in the evenings I had to rush out to the meetings.

Medical doctors, great friends of mine said, "Samuel, we have a solution, come to the hospital."

I had never been in the hospital a day in my life, but because I was so tired, I consented. They gave me a room in the hospital. They put a guard outside the door. Nobody could see me all day. I would get up in the evening, take my shower, and get ready for the meetings. Then I would go to the tent, preach, lead souls to the Lord, and go back to the hospital. I slept so well in that hospital!

* * *

One night during the tent meeting, a man came forward at the close of the service with tears in his eyes. He asked me, "Do you remember me?" I had no idea who he was. I have prayed for so many people that I can't possibly remember them all! He hung his head and said, "I slapped you!" It was my old boss, the Armenian cobbler who hired me when I was just a boy.

"Please forgive me now!" he begged.

"Not now!" I said. Then I smiled and added, "I don't need to forgive you now. I forgave you the day it happened."

Years before, he had left Jerusalem and moved back to Armenia. Now he was visiting Beirut. He saw the signs advertising the meetings. He came to see me out of curiosity, but during the meeting God touched him and that night he was gloriously saved.

Glory to God! He is a God of mercy!

25

Bible School and Christian Day School

I have always had a heart for children who have to leave school because they do not have enough money to get an education. I had to leave school when I was only 14, so while I was working in that shoemaker's shop, I vowed to the Lord, "One day when You bless me, I will open up a school for poor boys and girls and will never refuse any child because they do not have enough money to pay their school fees."

Fifteen years after I prayed that prayer, God began to give me a vision for a Bible School and Christian day school in Lebanon. I saw the land, I saw the buildings, I saw the students, and I saw the teachers. God made it so real and gave me such faith that I knew He was going to fulfill that vision.

One morning in the midst of our tent meeting revival, I was praying when God gave me a vision of a beautiful piece of property and told me, *This is the land for your Bible school.* My heart was filled with joy. I praised God for this promise. I went to share the good news with Naomi. We were a young family then. She was only 22 and I was 27 and we had two small children: Paul was four years old, and Jasmine was a baby. When I told my wife about the vision, she got very quiet. Even though she did not say anything, I could tell what she was thinking: *We are struggling just to put bread on the table. How can you even think about buying land for a school?*

But I sensed the Holy Spirit guiding me. I got in the car and started driving. The Holy Ghost directed me at each fork in the road. Eight miles north of the city, I came upon the land I had seen in my vision. It was beautiful. I got out of the car. There was a tall fence all around the property. I called out to see if anyone was there, but no one answered, so I climbed over the iron gate. I was looking around the place when the gardener came around the corner. He was startled when he saw me, but because of my clerical garb, he was too polite to say anything. I asked him, "Who owns this land?"

He hesitated.

I gave him a few Lebanese lira.

"Mr. Kattany owns this property."

Mr. Kattany! He was one of the richest men in the city. Everyone knew about Mr. Kattany.

I drove back into town, went to his building, and took the elevator up to his floor. I knocked on the office door. His secretary answered.

"I would like to see Mr. Alfred Kattany," I said.

"He's busy right now," she replied.

"I'll wait," I said. I sat down in the reception room. I waited 20 minutes, then Mr. Kattany graciously welcomed me into his office.

I introduced myself, then said that I was interested in buying his land. "This morning, God showed me a vision of your land. I have gone out to the property and it is exactly what I need to build a Bible school. I would like to buy the property."

Mr. Kattany smiled.

He thinks I'm rich, I thought. My whole life people have assumed that I am rich. My secret is that I act like the son of the King of Kings, and this makes everyone think I must be rich.

Mr. Kattany brought out a map of the property and showed me its size and where the borders lay.

"This is just what I need," I said. "How much do you want for it?"

"Because you are going to use the land for Christian work," he said, "I will sell it to you for a special price."

I nodded, to acknowledge his graciousness.

"There is also no real estate agent involved so we do not have to pay anyone commission. This will lower the price further. He wrote on a piece of paper, "330,000 Lebanese liras," and pushed the sheet of paper across his desk toward me. 330,000 Lebanese liras! That was an enormous amount in 1957. To give you some idea of how much money this was, back then our family was living on two hundred Lebanese liras a month—including rent and all our expenses. So 330,000 liras was enough to support our family for over one hundred years!

I looked at the paper with 330,000 Lebanese liras written on it and thought, *O Lord, how will I ever have this much money?*

"How much will you be able to put down on the property?" Mr. Kattany asked.

I looked up at him. "I agree that the price is fair. In fact, it is a very good price, but I have no money!"

Mr. Kattany looked at me. He was a successful businessman, over 70 years old and I was a young penniless priest in his twenties. "You have no money?" he asked. "You have no money and yet you are wasting my time talking about wanting to buy my land!"

"Mr. Kattany," I said with confidence, "Money does not bring faith, but faith brings money—and I have faith."

He looked startled at my boldness.

"Have you heard of tithing, Mr. Kattany?" I asked.

"No," he hesitated. "What is that?"

"The Bible," I replied, "teaches that whatever we earn, we must give one tenth of our income to God."

"What do you mean?" he asked.

"Look at the amount. The tithe, 10 percent of 300,000, would be 30,000."

"That's right," he said.

"Well," I said, "This 30,000 belongs to the Lord. If you will give me that money, then I will give it to you as a down payment."

Mr. Kattany covered his face with both hands and rubbed his eyes.

I watched him closely.

Then he looked at me and said, "I have never done anything like this before in all my life, but I like you. I am going to do this."

He quickly called his top secretary and began to dictate the terms of the sale, a full page of legal terms. He got out the legal stamps worth three hundred Lebanese liras and put them on the document. These stamps are a form of tax that made the sale legal.

With his 30,000 liras and his three hundred liras in tax I bought the land. We both signed the agreement and he gave me a key to the iron gate and keys to the three buildings on the property. According to the agreement, I would pay him 50,000 liras every six months for the next three years—with no interest.

I was shouting, "Hallelujah," as I drove home. How great is our God! To Him be the glory forever and ever.

Later that year, we opened Ebenezer Bible School, a boarding school with 27 students from Lebanon, Syria, Iraq, Iran, Egypt, and Greece. In a short time we had a day school with three hundred students in kindergarten, elementary school and high school.

26

Brazil and Beyond

By the late 1950s, invitations to preach began to pour in from Europe, the Americas and Africa. In 1957, during the revival in Beirut, God took me to the Sudan, Ethiopia, Kenya, and Uganda. In the late fifties and early sixties, I preached in 46 different states in the U.S., as well as Canada, from east to west and north to south. I traveled across North America, glorifying the name of the Lord, and seeing many precious souls come to the Lord Jesus.

In 1961, the Spirit of the Lord led me to Sao Paulo, Brazil, where I preached to the Armenian people in a place called Santana, which is a District of San Paulo. Once I was there, a Baptist church invited me to preach to the Portuguese-speaking Brazilians. Then the Presbyterians invited me, followed by the Pentecostals, and the largest Methodist church in San Paulo. Instead of staying three weeks as I had planned, I stayed five months, preaching daily. By the time I left, I was preaching to 25,000 in the great Maracana Stadium in Rio de Janeiro. To God be the glory.

* * *

While I was in Brazil, the Holy Ghost began leading me to preach on television. I told the campaign organizers, a committee of seven Brazilian men, that I thought I was supposed to preach on television.

"It's impossible," they said. "Evangelicals are not allowed to preach on television in Brazil."

"That word 'impossible!' is not in my vocabulary!" I insisted. "I don't believe in it. With God all things are possible."

The four of us went to a television station. We explained that we wanted to buy time on the station. The first question they asked me was, "Are you a Catholic Priest?" With my black suit and clerical collar, people often think I am a Catholic priest. I said, "No. I am a Christian evangelical preacher."

"Father," they said. "We are very sorry but it is strictly forbidden. Our Cardinals would be very angry. We cannot give you permission."

When we came out of the station, the three brothers said, "We told you!"

I said, "I am not giving up. Let's go to another station."

We went to Channel Nine.

They did not ask me if I was a Catholic priest. They assumed I was one.

"How long would you like this time slot, Father?" they asked.

"Three months."

"That will cost a lot of money."

"I don't mind." I wanted to sign the contract before they found out that I was not a Catholic priest.

They prepared the contract and we signed it. The first program was scheduled for next Sunday afternoon from 3:30 to 4:00. We left the television station leaping with joy.

Some of the brothers doubted. "They might find out that you are not a Catholic priest," they said. "They might stop you."

I did not have one little doubt. On Sunday, I went to the station. The director of the TV station was there. While I was preaching, I watched him out of the corner of my eye to see how he was reacting. When I looked, he was wiping away tears with his handkerchief.

I praised God. When I finished preaching, the station director came on television. He said to the TV audience, "This program continues next Sunday. Tell everybody you know to watch it."

I said, "To God be the glory!"

When we went home, my telephone rang. The manager from the first TV station asked, "Would you like to come back? We would like to speak with you again."

A company even called and asked if they could advertise on my show. They offered to pay me $20,000, if I would let them advertise liquor before and after I preached. I said, "You can keep your $20,000. I shall preach against liquor."

The Lord blessed me in Brazil. One Sunday afternoon, I fell on my knees, right there in the studio, as the cameras rolled, and said, "Everyone who wants to give your heart to the Lord, kneel down now, wherever you are."

That evening, I preached in the Presbyterian Cathedral, the largest church in Sao Paulo. During the offering someone put a calling card in the plate. The card said, "Isaac Franco." On the back of the card he had written, "Please come and visit me at my home. I must see you."

When my committee saw it, one of them, a judge, said, "Samuel, he is one of the richest men in Sao Paulo."

"To God be the glory," I said. I love to meet rich people. Not for their money. I am richer than they are. I have all the riches of my heavenly Father. But I love to see them come to God.

I took a few brothers and went to visit the man in his beautiful mansion the next day. He made us sit down while he stood. He said, "Forgive me, I speak better standing." Then he continued, "Yesterday, I was in front of my television set. I was listening to a program. I saw a priest speaking. I changed the channel, but as it flipped, I heard this priest shouting. I wondered, *What kind of priest shouts? What is he shouting about?* I turned it back again. It was you preaching, and when you asked us to kneel down, I fell on my knees right there." He began to cry. "I gave my heart to Jesus yesterday afternoon."

My heart was so moved.

Then he asked me, "Where is your wife and family?"

"In Lebanon," I said.

He said, "I want to bring them all here." He paid all the expenses to bring my wife, and my children—Paul, Jasmine, and Danny from Beirut to Brazil. He even brought the children's nurse. He paid for everything. He furnished a beautiful apartment overnight and gave it to us for our use. He also paid what remained of my three-month contract with the radio station. We stayed in Brazil many months preaching the glorious Gospel of our Lord.

I preached for only three months on television in Brazil, but God used that short time to change the hearts of the Brazilian authorities. After that, the restriction against Protestants was lifted and all over Brazil Protestants were allowed to preach on television. Today there are many preachers on television in Brazil, and some even have their own radio stations.

The Holy Ghost is still moving in Brazil. The revival fire that began with a few Armenians spread among the precious Portuguese-speaking Brazilians. To God be the glory!

27

To the Nations

From Brazil the Lord took me down to Montevideo, the capital of Uruguay, and Buenos Aires, the capital of Argentina, where again precious souls found the Lord Jesus as their personal Savior as revival fires burned in many churches.

I began to get invitations to preach from all over the world. In 1959 I went to Europe, where I preached in Switzerland, Germany, Holland and the Scandinavian countries. In the 1950s and 1960s, I made hundreds of trips to the U.S.A. I went all over Africa, from Cairo to Cape Town. I went to Asia including Indonesia and Malaysia, Singapore and Taiwan, Burma and the vast country of China. I preached in Australia. The Lord was fulfilling the prophecy He had given me in Jerusalem, when He said to me, "Lo, I go with you always." Hallelujah!

* * *

Now I travel almost continually. Some years I keep track. One year I held 532 meetings and slept in 137 different beds. As of today, I have traveled to 127 countries. I have been in so many airplanes that some call me the "Eagle of the Lord." When I travel, I never buy a first class ticket. I travel second class, only because there is no third class! But I still arrive at exactly the same time as the first class passengers. But sometimes the Lord spoils me.

In August of 1992, I was flying from Cyprus to Bahrain on my way to Singapore. I arrived at the airport and gave the lovely lady behind the counter a big smile. She smiled back, and then took my ticket. Her supervisor came and the two of them were speaking in a language I did not understand, but I could tell that they were talking about me. Then the first lady handed me a first class boarding pass! I gave her another big smile.

I was so happy! I was going to be flying Gulf Air, a rich oil-country airline, first class! I went to the first seat in the plane thinking to myself, *Three and a half hours. Fantastic. I am going to enjoy myself, eat wonderful food, and relax.*

Soon the plane started filling up. A young man from India sat next to me. He looked like a rich businessman. I looked at him and thought, *It is time to fish. If I throw the net and he slips out, I have enough time to throw it again. I have three and a half hours—and he cannot get away.*

We chatted for a bit. I could tell that he was well educated and from a high-class family. After we had gotten acquainted, I turned to him and asked, "What is your religion? Do you have a religion?" He lowered his head as if he were a bit ashamed, and then answered my question.

To make him feel more comfortable, I said, "You know, I am not a religious man."

His eyebrows shot up. He looked at my black suit, my clerical collar, and my cross, and then asked, "Not religious?"

"Not religious," I confirmed. "But I have heard about a Person, the greatest Person ever born. I have fallen in love with Him. I believe everything about Him. I am fascinated by His birth. I love His life. I love the words He spoke. I love the miracles He did. When I began to read about the miracles He performed, and the words He spoke and the life He lived, it attracted me. I love the way He let them kill Him. I love Him. They buried Him but He rose from the dead. He is alive. I'm following Him. I am not religious man, but I believe in that one Person. His name is Jesus."

His dark brown eyes followed every word I spoke. He was fascinated. Then I said to him, "In your religion do you believe that when you die, you come back again?"

He lowered his head again and answered, "Yes."

I knew what his religion believed, they believe that when you die, you can come back as a donkey. Imagine coming back as a donkey! Or you can come back a fly or a mosquito and get squashed just like that. *Splat!* Or come back as an elephant. They call this belief reincarnation. Millions in India and that part of the world believe in reincarnation.

I did not know what to say. I thought, *Lord, please give me inspiration. Give me wisdom. Give me the right words. I want to tell him something that will bring life. Something he will never forget. Please help me.* I was silent for one minute, two minutes. I didn't say a word.

I could tell that he was wondering why I was so quiet. I was thinking, meditating, listening to God. Then the Holy Spirit gave me a glorious answer. I said, "You know young man, when you die, or when I die, when we open up our eyes on the other side, and find ourselves in the presence of the Lord, we won't want to come back. We are in the presence of the Creator of heaven and earth. We won't want to leave. Maybe if you end up in that other place—I meant hell, but I did not say it—then coming back as a donkey sounds good. But not to me."

He looked at me as if lightening had struck. He pointed his finger at me and cried, "You're right! You're right. You're right!"

It was marvelous to see the Holy Spirit working in that young man. Before the plane landed, I had taken his hand in mine and led him to the Lord Jesus Christ. To God be the glory!

When we arrived in Bahrain, he didn't want to leave. He was going on to India, and I was going on to Singapore. He didn't want to part, but I could feel the touch of the Lord on him in such a marvelous way. I knew the Lord would be with him.

This is the greatest miracle of God: to be born-again by the Spirit of God. In America, when healing comes, everybody rushes to get healed, but physical healing is temporary. It only endures while we are on the earth. The greatest miracle of all is to be born-again by the Spirit of God. A child of the devil instantly becomes a child of God. You are in darkness; suddenly not only are you *in* the light, you become light! It is a miracle!

28

Traveling the Bible Lands and the World

Many people wonder how I started Bible Land Mission. The seeds for our mission go back to 1947, when I spent the night praying in the Garden of Gethsemane. I was only 17 years old, so I told my mother not to worry about me and went out alone to the Russian Orthodox Church compound in the Garden. At 9:00 in the evening I knelt at the foot of one of the olive trees and began to pray. I stayed there nine hours. The Lord was very near. I felt His presence. He gave me a burden for the Middle East.

Many years later, in 1956, I started a Spirit-filled international interdenominational society called Bible Land Mission. It was the fulfillment of the vision God gave me in the Garden of Gethsemane when I was only 17.

Our mission society is made up of born-again Spirit-filled Catholics, Orthodox, and Protestants. We bring churches of different denominations together in every country. My board of directors come from many denominations. We minister to Jews, Turks, Arabs, and Armenians. We still support our orphan families in Beirut and have three evangelistic centers that God has helped us establish. We hold revival meetings all around the world. Millions have been blessed through the Mission's ministry.

I have been all around the world, and I can say with confidence that the Bible land countries are some of the most difficult mission fields in the world. At times it is so hard that it seems impossible, but with God all things are possible. In the last 60 years, by the grace of God, I have seen the greatest move of God in those Bible land countries, where thousands have turned to the Lord Jesus Christ.

* * *

People ask me, "What is the secret of your strength? How can you travel year after year, holding meetings every day, sometimes twice a day?" I sleep in so many different beds that when I awake in the morning, it takes me half a minute to figure out where I am. I wonder, *What side of the bed can I get out on? Where is the door of this bedroom? And, where is the light?*

How do I keep going? The Holy Spirit, the Comforter, gives me strength. The Bible says, "He shall come upon you." This is not theory. This is not theology. This is not doctrine. This is an experience. You can experience it, too. The Third Person of the Trinity can live in you.

* * *

In every country, the people are different. Their temperament is different. Their reactions are different. Their faces look different. Their culture is different. Their languages are different. The way they worship is different. Some places are so lacking in zeal that you feel that you have entered into a refrigerator. And some places you feel that you have entered a fiery furnace.

I use interpreters in many countries as I preach the Word of the Lord. I have to keep my sentences short, and speak in such a way as to make it easy for the interpreter. I have to teach the right message for the right people. It isn't easy, but the Lord helps me in every situation.

I speak Arabic, but I am much freer in English, so when I preach to the Arabs, I use interpreters. I have used more than 30 different Arabic interpreters, but the greatest, the best is one I call the King of Interpreters. His name was Ezzat Attieh and he was an elder in a Presbyterian church in Cairo and the leader of our Soul Salvation Society in the land of Egypt.

He was incredible. I sweat when I preach. He didn't sweat, but when I took my handkerchief out to wipe my forehead, he would take his handkerchief out also and wipe his forehead, even though he didn't sweat. When I raised my voice or raised my hands—whatever I did—he did the same. It was tremendous. He interpreted every word, every sentence.

He did such a great job that we flew him to Australia one January so he could interpret for me in Sydney while I preached to the Egyptians and Lebanese. It was in 1989, and back then, there were four hundred thousand Lebanese living in Sydney as well as thousands of Egyptians. He did a fantastic job.

This dear brother is a few years older than I am. For many years he was not married. Many of our leaders in Egypt were not married. I persuaded all of them to marry. So many of them got married. We had a revival of marriages! The King of Interpreters named his first son Samuel. We love that baby. Many in Egypt have named their babies after me. There are hundreds of Samuels all over Egypt.

We have kept in touch over the years. I used to call him at his home in Alexandria. That last time I called I felt such a burden to contact him. He was sick. I prayed for him on the telephone. Then, a short time later, in the fall of 2005, he died.

A good interpreter must be full of fire. If he is frozen, you can preach full of zeal and anointing, but the message will come out frozen. When the interpreter and the preacher have fire, two are better than one, just like it says in the Bible.

* * *

I love to read the Scriptures. When I am preaching, I ask people to stand when I read from the Word of God. In my travels, I have seen many religious leaders, many temples of different religions. I've read their holy books, but there is nothing like the Word of

God. It is an incomparable book. In English we call it the Bible, the Holy Scriptures, or the Word of God. But in Armenian, we call the Bible *Asdvadzashountch*, which means "breath of God." If you want God to breathe on you, read His Word.

* * *

I thank God that He has given me an international stomach. It is a great blessing. No matter where I am, when they bring me food, I don't ask questions. I do what Jesus says to do in Luke 10:8: "eat such things as are set before you" (NKJV). I enjoy the food. It is delicious. I have learned that the moment you ask, "What am I eating?" you will wish you had not asked!

In some countries, of course, they eat with a knife and fork. In some they eat with chopsticks. I can eat with chopsticks. In some countries they think, *Why should we eat with knife and fork or chopsticks, when God has given us wonderful hands with five fingers that can move so well?* So they eat with their hands.

Once I was in a village in Jordan. The people were so happy that I was coming to their village. I had led many of them to the Lord, so they held a big celebration for me. They had made a famous dish called *mansaf*, which is lamb and rice on a big platter. The lamb is beautifully done, and laid on top of the rice. I sat down to eat and there in front of me was a little plate, knife, and fork. I looked around. I was the only one who had eating utensils.

I asked my host, "What's this for?"

"That's for you," he replied.

"What about you? How are you going to eat?"

"We eat with our hands, but we want you to use these. Take whatever you want and eat."

"No sir!" I took the knife and fork and put it aside. "I shall eat like you do."

I am glad they prayed. I prayed, too. I prayed, "Lord, help me!"

They washed their hands, I washed my hands, too. They pulled their sleeves up, and I did, too. I said to one of the dear brothers,

"You go first." He put his fingers in the rice, took a big portion, and began to form it into a ball. He put his thumb under it, opened his mouth wide, and flicked his thumb. It sailed through the air and landed in his mouth! Now they all turned to look at me. If I ever prayed, I prayed that day, "Help me, Lord!" I took little rice, just a little, made a small ball, just in case I missed. I rolled it, making it as hard as I could. Then I put my thumb under it and brought it close to my mouth. I was not cheating, just trying to use wisdom. Then I opened my mouth very wide, and I threw it. Thank God, it fell in my mouth!

They were so happy that I could eat like them. You know, when you put your fingers in that bowl and feel the oil and the rice, you get strange feelings all over, but soon, you begin to enjoy it.

One time in Ethiopia, the daughter of a tribal king brought me a bowl of soup. I was sitting by myself while all the men watched me from the window and the door, to see if I would like the food their princess had made for me. As the princess served me, I looked up and saw all those faces. I prayed, put my spoon in the bowl of soup, and put it in my mouth. It burned! My lips, my tongue, and my throat were burning. I prayed, Lord, help me! I prayed Mark 16:18, reminding God of His promise that if we drink any deadly thing, it will not harm us.

I took another spoonful. *Lord, help me! Help me!* I ate the whole bowl of soup. When I finished, everybody was clapping. You could tell that they were thinking, *Our princess is a wonderful cook.* Then I said, "Some more, please." She gave me some more. From those two bowls, I suffered three days. But never mind. It is wonderful to travel all over the world and enjoy the customs and culture of God's people.

Samuel with his brothers—(left to right) George, Samuel, Philip, and David

Samuel with his father, Mr. Boghos (Paul) Doctorian, at the age of eight

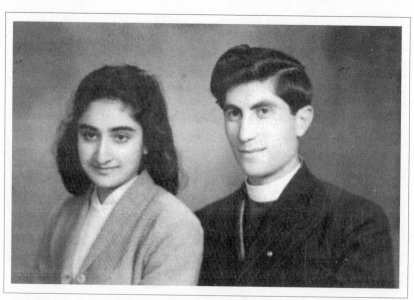

Samuel and Naomi (Pashgian) Doctorian

Samuel and Naomi in Jerusalem, 1954

Samuel, Naomi and their son, Paul, in Jerusalem

The Rev. Samuel Doctorian family—(clockwise from top left) Naomi, Jasmine, Paul, Daniel, Luther, Samuel and Samuel Jr.

Samuel in Jordan, on the way to Petra

Tent meetings in the U.S.A.

Samuel preaching in the Westminster Central Hall, London, England

Revival Meetings in Portugal

A day of Pentecost in Holland, where 2000 received Baptism of the Holy Spirit at the same time

Eleven thousand Hindus in India

Meetings in Siberia, 2003

Cape Town, South Africa, at the Apostolic Faith Mission

Mount Ararat, Armenia

In Armenia

The Peniel headquarter buildings of Bible Land Mission, Mansourieh, Lebanon

Entrance of Peniel, headquarters of Bible Land Mission in Lebanon

Golghotha, 2005

Carrying the cross on the way to Golgotha

125 days of fasting and praying on the Island of Patmos, where 5 Angels appeared to Samuel with the prophecies

The original shoe shop in Jerusalem, where Rev. Doctorian first received the call of the Lord

Celebrating 50th Anniversary with Naomi

The Doctorian Family—August 2006. Seated (left to right)—Sam and Arpy, Naomi and Samuel, (on lap, Rachel, Julia, and Joshua), Rebeca and Luther. Standing (left to right)—Jonathan, Paul, Tanya, Takouhi, Samuel, Nora, Dan, Noelle, Jasmine, Jennifer, Terry, and Benjamin.

29

Revival in Portugal

I met Billy Graham for the first time in 1955 at his great crusade in Glasgow. A few years later I saw him at another crusade in New York, but it was not until I saw him at his daughter's wedding in 1963, that we had a chance to talk at length. His daughter, Gigi, was marrying a young Armenian man whose family lived in Switzerland. I was invited to the wedding because I was a friend of the groom's family—the Tchividjian family.

A few days before the wedding, I was seated in the living room of the lovely Tchividjian home praying. My host, Brother Ara, knelt in front of me, took my hands and placed them on his head. He asked me to pray that God would fill him with the Holy Spirit. I prayed and sensed a great anointing.

Then he told me that Gigi was upstairs in bed with a high fever. The whole household was concerned. Several times a day the Grahams were calling from North Carolina to see if their dear daughter was better. No one knew if the wedding would go forward as planned or would have to be postponed.

"Brother Ara," I said, "Why don't you ask Gigi, would she like to be anointed with oil?"

"Good idea," he said. He went upstairs and spoke with Gigi. She was willing.

I went up. Her face was red hot with fever. I knelt beside her and anointed her forehead with oil. I laid hands on her and asked God to heal her. I could feel the fever leaving her through my hands. The Lord touched Gigi, and healed her perfectly.

Brother Ara called Billy Graham in North Carolina and told him that Gigi was healed completely.

"What happened?" he asked. They told Dr. Graham, "A man of God, Samuel Doctorian, is here. He anointed her with oil and prayed, and the Lord healed her."

At the wedding reception Billy Graham asked me to pray, then later he came up to me and asked me if he could speak to me privately. We agreed to meet the next day. One of the first questions he asked me was, "I've heard that you have had revival in Portugal. How did get in? I've been trying to get into Portugal for years and they won't let me in."

He was right. Portugal is a very hard country to reach. Almost everyone is Roman Catholic; Protestants make up only about 1% of the population. Back then the country was under a dictator who severely limited personal freedom. No one was allowed to use stadiums or theatres for political or religious gatherings. In addition, the few Protestant churches that were there were not united. They rarely spoke to each other. Each church seemed focused on building its own little kingdom.

A few years before I first went to Portugal, in the late 1950s, God led a Portuguese businessman to start a nondenominational Christian businessmen group in Lisbon. For the first time, Christians of different denominations began to spend time together. They had dinner parties together. They got to know each other. For the first time, we began to see unity among the different denominations.

That same group of Christian businessmen invited me to come and preach. They called me to come because they felt that God had something to tell them, something that they needed to hear and that I was the person who should deliver that message.

I had been in Lisbon before, for just two days in March 1962. God had greatly blessed those meetings. Now they wanted me to come again, but I was very busy. It was December 1962, before I was able to give them a date. I sent word that I would come again in February. They immediately organized a committee with representatives from all the Protestant denominations. They also invited an American missionary, Brother Fairchild, the director of the Baptist Seminary in town, to train counselors and to organize follow-up work for new converts. He had experience with evangelistic campaigns from working with Youth for Christ in Portugal.

Meanwhile there were many disagreements about how things should be done. Over and over again, the committee had to pray that their Heavenly Father would give them unity and divine guidance. They decided to hold the meetings in the three largest Protestant churches in Lisbon. They trusted that God would give them a bigger place as the attendance increased.

I arrived on January 31, 1963, and our first meetings were held in the Presbyterian, Assemblies of God and Episcopal Churches—each one alternating as host. God richly blessed those meetings, and every day more people came. The churches were packed, and during the first 10 days alone, some two hundred souls came to Christ. God had begun his work in Lisbon. Glory to His Name!

The spirit of unity among the churches was tremendous! The revival grew. Soon we needed a bigger place to meet. One of the major automobile dealerships in Lisbon was building a new showroom in the center of Lisbon. It was a huge hall, which had not yet been occupied. The president of the Christian Businessmen's group, a medical doctor named Bastos Goncalves, said to the owner of the building, "If you let us use your hall for our meetings, God will bless you!"

The owner let us use the building for 11 days, rent-free. But we had no chairs. We asked the municipality, and they gave us two thousand folding chairs to use, free of charge. Someone offered us the use of a sound system and all the lights free of charge. We got a great deal on a rented organ. All of this in a land where Protestants are a tiny, often ignored minority. God Himself had prepared the way.

Eighteen days after I arrived, we moved into the big hall. Normally, it could hold about two thousand people, but on the opening night there were three thousand people. Every seat was taken and people were jammed in the aisles and in every conceivable space. The hall began to fill hours before the meetings began. Crowds packed the place day after day. Thousands and thousands who had never heard the Word of God came to faith. God brought them all.

Many became convicted of their sins. Many were troubled and could not sleep at night. Hundreds came forward day after day to give their lives to Christ. It was wonderful to see tears of regret and conviction change into tears of joy and peace when they received Jesus Christ into their hearts.

After 62 days of meetings, the governor sent a message demanding that I stop preaching. The pastors said, "Samuel if you do not stop, they will put you out of the country and we will be in trouble."

That night I stood in front of the congregation. I did not know what to do. *No preaching!* So I began to pray. I was not preaching, but it was the longest public prayer I have ever said. I prayed as long as I usually preached. The crowd was saying, "Amen," and crying. That night more people were saved than when I preached.

The next morning, I went early to see the governor. I asked him why he was making me stop.

"It's not me!" he insisted. "It is the Cardinals. They are concerned that if you keep preaching, the whole country will become Protestant."

There was nothing I could do! I left Portugal. After that they would not let me back into the country.

Years later, the government of Portugal changed. The dictator was overthrown and democracy was restored. By now I was also an

American citizen. I no longer needed a visa to go to Portugal, so I went back. We had even greater meetings than before. To this day the revival fires are still burning in Portugal.

To God be the glory!

30

$\mathcal{M}$iracle Water

In 1960 we began holding evangelistic meetings in a garage in Beirut. After a month we had outgrown the garage and moved up to the second floor of a building in the Bourj-Hammoud neighborhood of Beirut. God blessed our ministry, which we called *Salem Evangelistic Center*. Hundreds of souls came to know Christ as their personal Savior. Many were wonderfully healed by the power of the Lord. Many were baptized with the Holy Ghost and with fire. Great things began in that Salem Center that spread all over the Bible lands.

After two years, God gave us a vision for our own church and provided the money we needed to buy a piece of land in the heart of Beirut. We had to wait several years before we could start the building project because we had many burdens in the mission work. We were supporting many orphans and paying the school fees of many poor children. But in 1968, by the grace of God, I felt God leading us to begin building.

We changed the blueprints four times. Each time the architect patiently made the changes. The night before we were going to break ground, the Spirit of the Lord moved on me in the night and told me I should build a basement under the entire building.

In the morning, I called in the architect and the engineer and told them what the Lord had revealed to me during the night.

They looked at each other and then at me and said, "Dear Brother, building a basement is impossible—and useless! It will be a waste of money to build a basement in that section of Beirut."

"Why?" I asked.

"It is so near the seashore. In the winter, every basement in that area fills with water. No one can use their basement. The only reason they built them in the first place is because the government used to insist that every building have a basement shelter. But now the law has changed and you don't have to build a basement anymore. Why do you want us to build a basement that will be full of water in winter, and not even useful in summer?"

I was not persuaded. I was so convinced that the Lord had spoken to me that I said, "I am sorry gentlemen. We must have a basement."

"It will cost you a lot of money," they said.

"That is not your concern. The Lord Who has led me to do this will supply the money. So please, let the bulldozers start digging. Change the plans so that we can have a huge basement under the church."

There was nothing they could say, so they made the changes and started digging.

When they got down 10 feet, the ground got muddy. Dirty water began to puddle on the surface. The bulldozer operators stopped working and protested that they could not continue working in the mud unless I paid them more money. We had to pay them more before they would continue digging.

They dug deeper and deeper. It got muddier and muddier. They brought in a pump to try to pump the water out, but no matter how much they pumped, it kept getting wetter.

One morning when I came to the site the whole place looked like a swimming pool. Everybody stood looking at it, not knowing what to do.

"Bring two pumps!" I said.

They tried to pump the water from the large basin of water and haul the mud away in trucks. It was very hard work. We continued this way for two days.

Then, one morning, when I was working in my office, the phone rang at about 10:00 A.M.. It was the engineer saying, "Come quickly and see what has happened!"

I did not understand what he was talking about, but I drove the five miles to the construction site as fast as I could. All the neighbors were gathered around the building site, watching.

God had done a miracle.

A fountain of crystal clear water was shooting up in the middle of the muddy pool. The workers had struck a spring in the middle of our property. That spring was the reason the basements in this part of town flooded each winter.

In the Middle East, water is more valuable than gold. We were filled with joy at the sight of all that water. The architect and the engineer, who had initially objected to building a basement, now said, "Look what we've found!"

"To God be the glory," I said, "that we have found this beautiful spring!" We built a well right in the middle of the basement, and we never had to buy water again. We even built our huge cement building using the water from the spring. We had all the water we needed—once again God had not failed us.

31

Revival in London

The Holy Ghost works in tremendous ways. Once, in the late sixties, we had two visitors from Hong Kong come to our mission in Beirut: a British lady missionary to Hong Kong, and a Chinese pastor named Steven Wong. Somehow they had heard of us and written to see if they could visit. We were delighted to have them.

Our Salem Evangelistic Center was still under construction when they arrived, but we had rented four adjacent apartments in nearby a building, and removed the interior walls to make a great hall that could seat six hundred. We also had two shops down below, at the street level, where we held smaller meetings. I asked Stephen Wong to speak on Palm Sunday. He preached in English, and I interpreted into Armenian for those who did not understand English.

When they were leaving, Stephen Wong asked, "Will you come preach to us in London? We have a Chinese church there that meets at the YMCA in London."

I preached in Wong's Chinese church in London on a Sunday afternoon to about two hundred. They invited me back. This time they took me to a different Chinese church in the center of London. One week became two. The second week people from other nations began to come. The third week we saw people from many countries. One night I asked one person from every nation to come stand on the platform with me. There were 54 countries represented in that meeting.

The next day, newspaper reporters came to the meeting, and the following day, the front page reported that people from many nations were worshipping together, just as they had in the day of Pentecost.

One night, over three hundred stood to be baptized with the Holy Ghost and with fire. I said to the congregation, "All those who are not standing, please leave now. I'm going to close the meeting. God bless you. Go home now." I sent everybody away except those three hundred who had stood.

Then I said to the three hundred, "Please come forward now." They all came and stood across the front to receive the mighty baptism of the Holy Ghost. There were Chinese, Scandinavians, Germans, Swiss, Indians, Pakistanis and people from many Far East countries. There were members of Parliament and church leaders from different denominations. I told them how to receive the Holy Ghost. I explained that first, you must be saved. Second, you must have a hunger for the Holy Ghost. Third, you have to dedicate totally your life to God. Everything needs to be on the altar. Fourth, you must ask the Lord to cleanse your heart from every sinful appetite. You must ask him to remove every sin from your heart. Fifth, you have to have faith that the Holy Ghost will come when you ask Him to come. You open your heart to the Holy Ghost and receive Him.

Once I gave the instructions, suddenly, everyone heard a rushing wind. We all heard it. Above all the traffic noise outside, we heard a mighty wind. It was tremendous. The Holy Ghost fell on all three hundred spontaneously. Instantly, everyone was filled with the Holy Ghost. If you have never felt the presence of God, I tell you there is nothing like it. It is not your imagination. It is not your emotions. It is real. You know that you are in the presence of Almighty God.

I remember one brother, a great businessman, a well-to-do fellow from Singapore, named Ng, who said, "I felt my feet lifted up. I was no longer standing on the earth."

Out of that meeting, 20 Chinese churches in England and Scotland were planted, as well as churches in Holland, Belgium, and France. That mighty revival started with those three hundred.

News of the revival spread to other members of Parliament, and they invited me to speak to the House of Commons. I said, "No, thank you. I preach in halls and churches and schools, but not to the members of Parliament. I am not preaching there."

The brethren said, "Samuel, this is a great privilege. Not every preacher is invited to preach in the House of Commons. You must do it."

"Well, I don't know what to say to those men."

Eventually they persuaded me and I accepted the engagement. I kept asking God to give me a message, but I did not hear anything.

Some of the brethren from the House of Parliament said, "We hope you are ready. Many people are going to come! You're speaking in the grand hall in the House of Commons."

"OH, LORD," I cried. "GIVE ME A MESSAGE!"

The Lord would not give me a message. So I thought, *All right. I know how to prepare a sermon. I'll prepare a beautiful introduction. I'll have a first, second, and third points. I'll have a good conclusion. I can preach.*

The Lord said, "Is that what you want to do? All right. Go ahead."

"No, no, no!" I said. "Without You I cannot do it. Give me a message!" Anybody can preach a sermon, but a message is not a sermon. A sermon can be a work of man, but a message comes from God. The day I was scheduled to preach, I still had no message.

That night, I met the chairman, a man named Cyril Black. He was tall. I'm short. I felt weak. He led me to the grand hall. As we walked down the aisle, I noticed that the place was packed. When I got to the front, I fell to my knees. "God," I cried, "give me a message now!"

I heard God speak to my heart, *Preach on that passage of scripture, 'I am not ashamed of the Gospel of Jesus Christ, for it is the power of God unto salvation to everyone that believes, to the Jews and to the Greeks.'* So I did.

My sister, Angela, was seated in the front row holding a tape recorder. We learned later that no one is allowed to record anything in there, but we did not know that so she recorded the whole message.

"British Government, Dominion Kingdom," I began. "There was a time when you had every country of the Middle East under your authority, but because you did not use the strongest weapon—the Gospel of Jesus—so the day came when one by one, these countries said to you, 'Britain, get out. Britain, get out. Britain, get out.'" I mentioned Jordan, Iraq, Palestine, Egypt, and Syria. All these countries were once ruled by Britain, but today, there are no British there, and those countries are still in darkness.

Later Cyril asked, "Will you allow us to make a copy of that tape?"

"Sure," I replied.

They transcribed the tape. They printed the message. They asked me, "What title shall we give it?"

"I don't know. You can choose any title you want," I replied.

On the cover of that little booklet, they put a drawing of dynamite exploding and they called that message, "The Dynamite of God: the Gospel of Jesus."

They sent it to the Queen and to every member of Parliament.

I thought they would never invite me again, but later on, to my surprise, they invited me back. This time I preached on the power of the Holy Spirit.

To God be the glory. The work of revival in London was tremendous. I give God the glory.

32

War in Lebanon

In April of 1975, civil war broke out in Lebanon. It was a terrible trial. No one would have predicted that war would come to that beautiful, peaceful country. But I knew. Some years before, God had warned me in a vision. It happened in 1968, during one of our tent meetings in Beirut. In the middle of the meeting, while I was preaching, the Spirit of the Lord suddenly took hold of me. I closed my eyes, and while thousands of people watched, I reported what I was seeing in the vision. I saw a dark cloud come out of the sea until it completely covered the entire city of Beirut. I saw smoke rising from every part of the city. I saw buildings destroyed and thousands of dead people lying in the streets. It was a terrible sight.

I told the people everything the Lord showed me. Everyone was shocked. Some questioned, and some said, "It can't be." The elders came to me and said, "Brother Doctorian, what terrible things you said about Beirut! Do you really think it is possible that something like that will happen to this beautiful city? It is such a thriving center of commerce. It is the center of banking and business in the Middle Easty. There is freedom in this country. It has a strong government and a good constitution. Lebanon has always been such a peaceful country. How can it be devastated? What you are saying is impossible!"

I knew what they said about Lebanon was true. Lebanon is on the boundary between Asia and Europe and has long been an international center of finance, trade, and transportation. Before the war, Beirut was known as the Paris of the Middle East. But I could not deny what God had shown me. I knew the vision was from God.

Some who loved and respected me very much, asked, "Don't you think what you saw in your vision will take place when Jesus comes?"

I said, "No. It is going to happen soon."

I went to the president of the country, Kameel Shamoun, a powerful man, who was also a personal friend of mine. I said to him, "God showed me the city of Beirut. It will be like Sodom and Gomorrah. Destruction is coming. We must repent and return to God."

We fell on our knees, he and his wife, along with another minister who came with me. We prayed, "Oh, God! Oh, God, remember Beirut!" But everything that the Lord showed happened.

* * *

In 1975, the vision was fulfilled. The dark cloud came over the city. Officials say that more than 144,000 people died. Nearly 13,000 were abducted and 17,000 are still missing. Thousands of buildings were destroyed. The war lasted 17 years, and in many ways the country still has not recovered. During the war, Lebanon was invaded by Syria and Israel. Israel did not leave southern Lebanon until the year 2000, and it was not until the spring of 2005 that the Syrians finally departed.

* * *

There was one bright spot in the war. When the enemy cut off the water supply to the city and poisoned the city's drinking water, we were able to supply water to hundreds of people from our Salem spring. Hundreds of people lined up in the streets waiting to fill their buckets at the spring in the basement of our building.

Our huge basement also become a shelter for over seven hundred people who huddled there during the nine days of heavy bombardment in 1979, when more than 100,000 bombs fell on our city. They praised God that He had led us to build that basement. Not one person was harmed even though I wondered at times if our building would be completely destroyed. Miraculously, not one bomb or shell hit our church. I bowed before God and praised Him for what He had done.

He is a God of miracles who will not fail! He knows our needs before we do. Glory to God!

To this day, the spring in the basement is still flowing. We have as much water as we need for the whole building. Isn't this the mighty work of God?

After the heavy bombardment, we completed the building and held a dedication service. People came from many parts of Europe and America. We named the building Salem Evangelistic Center. That day was a historic day, as we all held hands and dedicated the church. With tears we praised God, singing: "To God be the glory, great things He hath done!"

* * *

The war was treacherous. One faction fought against another: Maronite Christian, Shiite, Druze, and Muslim—all killing each other. At the time the war broke out, I had four sons of military age. All of the different factions, the militarized political parties, wanted to force my sons to fight for them. I tried to tell them, "We are Armenians. This is not our war! Our people had nothing to do with this war." But they would not listen. I decided that I had to get my boys out of the country.

My youngest brother, David, was a state senator in Missouri in the United States. I contacted him, and he helped me get visas for everyone but Paul. Paul was over 21 so we had to apply for his visa from within the U.S.A. We even got visas for my parents. We came to America, thinking, *In a few weeks or a few months, things will get better and we can go back to Lebanon.* But it only got worse.

It was terrible to have to leave Paul behind. We had to wait a year before we could get a visa for him to join us; and during that year, he lived alone in Lebanon.

At first we stayed in Zion, Illinois, with some dear Armenian friends. They were very hospitable, but I wanted my family to be settled. I spent the whole night praying, "Lord, where do You want us to go? Where shall we settle?" Through the night, the Lord led me clearly. He said, "Go West."

Danny was in the Mennonite High School in Virginia so we left him there. The rest of us flew to California, and then drove to San Luis Obispo where we had some Armenian friends. I had led the father of that family to Christ. We had so little money that I had to buy our tickets with a credit card. This man, a tailor, had two daughters about the same age as my daughter. I wanted my family to be near another Armenian family so they would not feel so alone while I traveled. I still had to travel the world to preach and raise money for our ministry, including the orphans in Beirut.

One day when we were going around the town, I saw a house for sale. I called them, and with a five hundred dollar down payment, I bought the house. By the grace of God, we were able to pay for it little by little. We lived in that house in San Luis Obispo for five years, from 1976 to 1981.

In 1981, we moved to Pasadena, California, where there is a large Armenian community. We started an Armenian Church of the Nazarene where my oldest son Paul later became the pastor. God has blessed us in Pasadena. To Him be the glory!

33

Fire Worshipper

In my travels I meet so many nominal Christians, so many people who are born into a Christian home but do not give their hearts to the Lord. I tell you, they are living in darkness. They are lost forever.

Once I was on a plane seated next to a person who was fingering a cigarette. I hate tobacco, and that is why I am so glad that today most airlines do not allow smoking on their flights. But it was not always that way. This was the early eighties, before such bans were in effect. As soon as the "No Smoking" light went off, the man started puffing smoke in my face. I could only hope he would soon be finished, but when the cigarette got near the end, he used the old one to light a new one! I wanted to move, but when I looked around the plane there were no empty seats.

I tried to ignore him. I thought, *Okay, you smoke. I'll read the Bible.* I took my Bible out of my brief case. When he saw my Bible, I could feel him bristle. I knew he was thinking that I must be a religious fanatic to be reading the Bible on an airplane.

I read a chapter, and then glanced at him.

His eye caught my eye, so I said to him, "How are you, Brother?"

He looked at me and said, "I am not your brother."

"Are you a Christian?" I asked.

He looked at me a little oddly. "Of course I am! What do you think I am, a heathen?"

"When did you become a Christian?" I asked.

"I was born a Christian!"

"Well," I said, "you are the first one I've ever met. Born a Christian."

"What were you born?" he asked. "A Jew?"

"No," I said.

"Muslim?"

"No."

"What were you born?" he asked.

"I was born a sinner. I had to be born-again to become a Christian."

"Well, I don't know about these things."

Imagine that! He thinks he's a Christian, but he doesn't know what it is to be born-again! Being a member of a certain church or denomination does not make you a Christian. Being born into a Christian home does not make you a Christian. Being a Christian begins with a miracle. It is a supernatural act of God. Nominal Christianity is not Christianity.

I told him some of my story, but I could tell that he did not enjoy hearing it. I looked at the teenage boy sitting next to him. "What about him? What is he?" I asked.

Somehow the man knew—perhaps because they were both from Iran. He replied, "He is a fire worshipper."

"What?" I asked.

"He's a fire worshipper."

"Would you change places with me, please?"

"What are you going to do?"

"That's none of your business," I replied. "Will you change places with me?" The man agreed. He got my aisle seat and I got the middle seat. I don't like to sit in the middle seat, but I wanted to talk to that boy.

I looked at him. He looked tense. "First time in an airplane?"

He nodded.

Looking out of the window. I said, "Isn't flying beautiful. It is safer up here than down there in a car." He looked at me and took a deep breath.

"I fly all the time," I said, trying to reassure him. "I love it. We are up above the clouds." We began to chat. I learned that he was 14 years old. I said to him, "What religion are you, Son?"

He looked at me and said, "We worship fire."

"I'd like to know," I said, "I am really curious, how do you do that?"

That precious boy said to me, "We have an altar in the middle of a great temple. Fire is always burning, 24 hours a day, and we fall down and pray to the fire."

I said to him, "Why do you do that? I'd like to know."

He said, "The day is coming when all the wicked and bad people are going to be burned forever and ever in fire. So we pray that we may not be burned in fire."

I said, "Have you heard about somebody named Jesus?"

"No."

"I want to tell you a story," I said. I just happened to have in my pocket a beautiful picture book on the life of Jesus that folded like an accordion. I took it out of my pocket. I began to show him the wise men. The shepherds in the field. The star over Bethlehem. You've seen those pictures before, but this boy had never seen them. I began to show him the miracles Jesus did, how the lame walked and the blind eyes were opened.

The boy was drinking in every word. Then I showed him how they nailed Jesus to the cross. The boy turned to me and his brown eyes filled with tears. "Why did they do that?" he asked. "What did He do?"

I had the answer. "He died so that we might be delivered from fire. There is a place called hell. In hell, there is a lake of fire and a place of outer darkness. There is a place where hands are bound, feet are bound and people are thrown into the outer darkness. There is a place where there is weeping and gnashing of teeth. This is all written in the Bible. That is the reason Jesus came. He came so we would not go to hell when we die. If we don't believe in Jesus before we die, then we find out too late that hell is real.

"But if we love Him and are born-again, then we are going to praise Jesus for ever and ever in a wonderful place called heaven, where God will wipe away every tear from our eyes. Up in heaven, God sits on His throne. It is all written in the Bible."

That precious boy listened so intently.

"Look, look!" I cried, pointing at the next picture. "Jesus died and they buried Him; see, this is His tomb, but look at the next picture—He came back to life! Hallelujah! The sky you are looking at, the clouds below us, and the sun over there are all controlled by Jesus. He rose from the dead. He defeated death.

"Right now, He is in this airplane. I believe in Him. I gave Him my heart. He changed my whole life. And if you want, He can change yours, too. Would you like to give your heart to Him?"

He did not hesitate. He had no second thoughts. "Oh yes!" he cried, with shining eyes.

I thought to myself, *This man on my left thinks he is a Christian, but he is lost forever. This precious boy was lost, but now he will be saved forever.*

I led him in a prayer. "Just repeat these words after me: "Lord Jesus."

When he said the words, "Lord Jesus," it sounded like music.

"Come into my heart."

He repeated after me, "Come into my heart."

I continued to lead him. "Your blood washed me. Forgive my sins. Save me from fire." He said it all. "In Jesus' name, Amen."

The moment he said, "Amen," he looked at me with tears in his eyes and said, "I am going to tell this story to my daddy and mommy."

I started to cry. The moment he hears the story, he wants to tell his father and mother!

I closed that beautiful picture book and said, "Can I give this to you?"

"You mean," he faltered, "I can have it?"

"Yes, it is yours." He took it from me like it was sacred. He put it in his pocket. I knew that as soon as he got home, he would tell his mommy and daddy.

I never saw this young man again. But I know that one day I will meet him again. Halelujah!

34

Bombs, Cars, and Bibles

The war in Beirut was very difficult for us. Even after I got my family out of Lebanon, I still had one hundred orphans in our building in Beirut. Our Peniel building is eight miles outside Beirut on the side of a mountain. *Peniel* means "face-to-face I have seen the Lord and won the victory." The word comes from the story in Scripture where Jacob wrestled with God. The building had more than one hundred rooms and housed our school, church, and orphanage. In addition to the orphans, hundreds of students studied in our school. We also had missionaries living in the building. During the war, I was very concerned about all of them.

Many times, bombs struck the building. In 1979, a Russian-made rocket went through three walls and landed in my bed at 6:23 in the morning. Thank God, I was not at home. My whole bedroom was burned, and I lost some very precious things, gifts from all over the world. Things that people had given to me. I used to lock that door so people would leave my room alone, so you can imagine how I felt when I lost everything in there.

But I was protected. The devil made a mistake. I was in Surabaya, Indonesia, preaching, so I was not hurt.

Two hundred rockets and bombs hit the building. It was devastating, but thank God, He protected us. They can destroy our buildings. They can break our windows. But they cannot destroy our faith! We rebuilt everything. My bedroom was completely reno-vated—new paint, new wallpaper, new furniture. It was better than before. We replaced the broken windows and repaired holes in the walls. If you were to come now, you would not be able to tell that rockets ever hit the building.

* * *

Once during the war, robbers broke into our Peniel building and robbed my children. I was out of the country, but Paul was staying in the mission. He had gone back to Beirut after a time in America and now he was the principal of our Peniel School. He had married and his wife, Takouhi, and my daughter, Jasmine, were there with him, helping out with the school.

That morning gunmen got into the building and robbed Paul, Takouhi, and Jasmine. They took Takouhi's wedding ring and en-gagement ring. They stole all the cash I had in the house to pay the teachers' salaries and locked the three of them in the bathroom.

The robbers had a get-away car outside, with another man at the wheel, and they raced away. Thank God, the gunmen didn't kill my children. It was a lawless time! People were being kidnapped and robbed, and there was no one to stop them.

Miraculously, that same afternoon, I arrived in Beirut. I was not scheduled to arrive for many days, but God intervened in a way that got me there that same day.

I say "miraculously" because that morning, I had been sitting on a ship in Athens harbor waiting to leave for Beirut. I was bring-ing a used car from Ireland to Cyprus. I had gotten as far as Greece and had put the car on a ship that was supposed to leave Athens that night. I had gone on board the ship and gone to bed, but dur-ing the night, I noticed that the ship was not moving. In the morn-ing, I saw that we had not left the seaport.

"What happened?" I asked the sailors.

"Mechanical trouble. We're not able to leave yet."

I didn't know what to do. I already had a room on the ship. The car was on the ship, but I felt in my spirit that the ship was going to be delayed a very long time. I was wandering around the seaport, when I got caught up with a group of American tourists who were leaving the port for Athens.

The customs officials assumed that I was part of the group, so they let me walk out of the seaport without checking my passport to see if I had a visa to enter Greece. I had already gone through customs and immigration to leave the country, so I could not get out of the harbor area without a new visa. But suddenly here I was, outside the port!

I was amazed. I had gotten back into Greece without a visa. I went straight to the Armenian shops. The moment the shopkeepers saw me they couldn't believe that I was standing in front of them.

I told them, "I don't know how long the ship will be delayed. I want to fly to Beirut. But I don't have a visa to be here, so I don't know how I am going to leave."

Then I remembered. The director of Middle East Airlines was a great friend of mine. I went to him and told him about my situation. He said, "Don't worry. We'll take care of everything." They took me to the airport, through a secret gate, and into the terminal where I got my boarding pass for Beirut. By 4:00 P.M. that day, I was in Beirut.

At the time I had no idea my children had just been robbed earlier that day. I only sensed an urgency to get back. As soon as I got to Beirut, and saw their pale faces, I knew something was wrong. I realized then that the Lord had led me to leave the ship and take a plane.

"What's wrong?" I asked them. They didn't answer my question until we were safely inside our home. Once we were inside our apartment in the mission building, they told me, trembling, "Daddy, a few hours ago, gunmen came and stole all our money and jewelry. It is a miracle they didn't kill us."

"Thank God they did not hurt you!" I cried. "Life is more precious than money. God will supply all the money we need."

It was a sad experience. My children were so shaken that I had to send them back to America. After that I moved everyone out of the building. I put the orphans in private homes around the city. I stayed there alone with my German Shepdherd dog, Lucky.

* * *

During the war in Lebanon, my beautiful new Ford Cortina was hit by a rocket from the Palestinian camp. I had just brought the car from Birmingham, England. The car was completely destroyed so we pushed it out of the way with a bulldozer and buried it. I was preaching in Texas at the time, and when the people there heard about it they decided to give me a car. When Texans do something, they do it big. This was a big, beautiful car, a Ford LTD. I didn't know what the "LTD" stood for, so I told everyone it meant, "Lent to Doctorian."

After I got that car, a minister asked if I would like to have a CB radio in my car. I didn't know what a CB radio was, so he explained that it was a radio that lets you talk to people while you drive. This was, of course, in the days before cell phones.

After I heard his explanation, I said, "I see. Put it in."

Then we had to register the radio and I had to come up with a "handle"—a name that I would use while I was on the air. I chose *dunamis*, which means "power" or "dynamite" in Greek. I explained to him how Jesus had said, "You shall receive power," to His disciples. What Jesus was really saying, "You shall receive dynamite!"

I had a great time talking to other drivers on my CB radio. People would ask, "What's your handle?" And I would say, "Dunamis." Then they would ask, "What's that?" It gave me an opportunity to explain that Jesus said we would receive power.

Some of them didn't talk to me after that.

One time I was driving along when a woman came on the air. "Dunamis, are you there?"

I said, "I'm right here. What's your handle, lady?"

She said, "Ding-a-ling."

Ding-a-ling, I thought. *I have never heard that before.* We began to talk and I told her, "I am preaching in the First Baptist Church this evening. Why don't you come?"

"I don't know."

"Why don't I give you the address?"

"I don't know," she hesitated.

That night the place was crowded. At the end of the service I was praying for everyone who had come forward. There was a large woman right in the middle of the group kneeling at the front. She was crying. She had given her heart to Jesus. She looked up at me and said, "Do you know who I am?"

"No," I shook my head.

"I'm Ding-a-ling."

I still don't know her real name. When I get to heaven, I will have to ask the angels, "Is Ding-a-ling here?"

* * *

During the terrible Lebanese war, thousands of Armenian Bibles were burned in the city of Beirut. Suddenly there were no more Armenian Bibles, not just in Lebanon, but anywhere in the world. As Armenians, we were very sad. I would meet Armenians during my evangelistic meetings and they would ask if I had any Armenian Bibles and I would have to say "No." In the past, I would just get their name and address and send them a Bible from Lebanon. It was terrible to have to say, "I am sorry, we have no more Armenian Bibles."

This went on for six years. It got harder and harder to find Armenian Bibles. It was difficult to understand why we could not have the Bible in our own language. Then, miraculously, the Lord led me to a publishing house that was willing to publish Armenian Bibles. In just over eight months we published 15,000 Armenian Bibles. We also published Bible studies and maps of the Holy Land. Today these Bibles are all over the world: in America, Europe, the Middle East, South America, and of course, Armenia.

The Lord has blessed Bible Land Mission by letting us take part in this tremendous ministry. We praise Him for it!

* * *

After I had lived in America for five years, I wanted to apply for citizenship, but there were certain requirements that made it impossible. I had my green card, my residency permit, and had been in the country for five years, but according to immigration law, you also have to stay in the country for a whole year without leaving. That was impossible! I am only home perhaps a total of two months a year—a week here, a week there—maybe, at most, a month at a time. I am always traveling, always going in and out of the country. I wanted to be an American citizen, but staying in the country a whole year was not an option.

Then a man from Kansas City heard a recording of one of my sermons. He loved my preaching. I learned that he was one of the directors of immigration. I had his phone number, so I called him. He was happy to hear my voice, and I told him about my situation. "I would love to be a citizen, but I can't stay in the country a whole year. I have a ministry and hundreds of orphans to support. I simply cannot take a year off!"

"Where are you?" he asked.

"I am in Pasadena, California, but my residency is in San Luis Obispo, where I used to live. I have to apply for immigration from that town."

"Give me some time," he said. "I will call you back."

In two hours, he called me back. He said, "Can you get to San Luis Obispo now?"

"Immediately!" I said. It is about three and a half hours' drive. I took my brother-in-law, and together we drove to San Luis Obispo, straight to the courtroom. We arrived about four o'clock in the afternoon.

When the judge saw me sitting in the back, he closed out the court case they were working on, and said, "Now, let's do something enjoyable."

He welcomed me and shook my hand. The secretary came in with all the paperwork. He asked me to raise my right hand and swear. I raised my right hand. But then I said to the judge, "Your honor I cannot swear; I have never sworn in my life."

He looked at me. "All right," he said. "You don't have to swear, just use the word, 'affirm.'"

"Very good," I said. I repeated the words he said, saying after each section, "I affirm." After we finished, the judge shook my hand and said, "I welcome you, dear brother, as a citizen of the United States of America."

He was a brother! The judge! A believer!

"Thank you, dear judge!" I said.

Then they prepared all the citizenship documents right there. Instead of mailing them to me, they handed them to me. The next morning I was in the Los Angeles passport office.

The lady behind the counter asked, "When did you become a citizen?"

"Yesterday."

"Where are your citizenship papers?" I handed them to her. I could tell that she was wondering how I got them so fast. In half an hour I was holding my American passport!

It was fabulous! When I had only a Lebanese passport, I had to have a visa for every country. It can be tortuous to get visas. Sometimes you have to wait for days—and they can be so expensive! American citizens don't have to have a visa for most countries. Now that I am an American citizen, I can travel so freely. I still have my Lebanese citizenship and I was recently granted honorary citizen of Armenia. However, you cannot travel easily with those passports, so having an American passport is a great blessing.

35

$\mathcal{V}$oyage on a Cattle Ship

About seven years after the war began, I was in Holland visiting a wealthy Dutch businessman named Peter, the owner of a large meat processing plant. His company butchered five thousand calves a week to supply first-class restaurants and hotels in Europe and the Middle East.

Long before the war started, Peter had adopted a boy from a hospital in Beirut. He was so happy to have that boy! Then he asked for a girl, and we found him a little girl to adopt.

That night we were eating dinner in his home. I was dining on a delicious filet mignon, when he asked me, "Samuel, when are you going back to Beirut?"

"Not now," I said. "The airport is closed and I don't want to go through Cyprus. The journey by boat is treacherous. Twenty hours by ship, in rough seas. I am going to wait until the airport opens."

"Samuel, the next time you go, let me know. I have friends who own a big supermarket in Beirut. I am going to telex $10,000 to that market to buy food for your orphans."

"I am going next week!" I cried. "I don't care how difficult the journey may be. $10,000 in food for my orphans!"

It was March of 1982. Right when I got there, there was a lull in the fighting. For the first time in days, the supermarket opened.

This was a miracle. Outside it was cold and windy, but I got a truck-load of food—rice, sugar, wheat. They had whatever you wanted in that store. Most of the food went to my orphans, but we also distributed 180 bags of food to the poor people in the city.

That night, I was exhausted, but happy. I went to bed thinking, *I'll wait a few more days and see if the airport opens so I won't have to go back by boat.*

The worst part of the war was that you never knew when the fighting would break out again. I hoped it would stay quiet and they would open the airport so I could fly out. But you never knew. One faction would ambush another and it would all flare up again as each side took revenge against the other.

At three o'clock in the morning, I felt somebody physically shaking me. I had been sound asleep, so at first, I didn't open my eyes. In my groggy state, I wondered, *Who is it?*

My first thought was, *It's a robber!*—because we had been robbed before, and even since, I had kept the building empty. I had moved all the orphans out of our building into private homes so they would be safe. I was the only one staying in the 140-room mission house. I was by myself with only Lucky, my big, beautiful German shepherd for company. Lucky would sit outside my door and whine as the bombs fell all around our three-story mission building.

So you can imagine my surprise when I felt someone shaking me in the middle of the night. In my half-asleep state, my first thought was that someone was robbing us again.

Then I was shaken a second time. I opened my eyes. It was a beautiful angel! In a clear voice, the angel said, "Rise, servant of the Lord. Prepare yourself. Leave Lebanon today."

I was struck by his words, "Servant of the Lord!" Even now, years later, when I remember those words, tears fill my eyes. An angel called me "Servant of the Lord!"

I rose, packed my bags, and called one of my pastors. He came with another man, a deacon, and together they drove me to the harbor. They seemed baffled that I was leaving so soon, but I knew that God had told me to leave. If you have never seen an angel, you might not understand, but it was such an overpowering experience that I wanted to hold it close to my heart. I did not tell them about my night visitor.

I purchased my ticket and we were waiting outside, when an announcement came over the loudspeaker. The ship would not be leaving as scheduled. It was too stormy. The winds were too strong. Trees were falling. The boat was some distance out from the harbor, and it was too dangerous to ferry us out there in small boats with the high seas.

I stood there, talking silently to God. "Lord, Your angel said to leave today. Surely You know about the weather. How am I supposed to leave, if the ship does not depart?"

One of the men with me lived near the seaport. "Pastor," he said. "Come and sleep at our house. We'll bring you back in the morning."

"No," I said, "Leave me alone for a few minutes. I'm meditating." I needed to hear from God.

Suddenly, there was another announcement: "A cattle ship will be leaving in two hours. Passengers may go on the cattle ship, if they like, but it is a freight ship, so there are no chairs or bunks."

I walked up to the ticket window and exchanged my ticket for one on the cattle ship. When the people in the waiting room saw me exchange my ticket, they decided that if the Father was going on the cattle ship, they would go, too. The entire crowd—about a hundred people—got in line to exchange their tickets.

When it came time to board, I helped the mothers and children onto the ship, and then climbed on myself. It was not easy to get everybody settled, as the ship was not set up to accommodate people.

The captain of the ship saw me on deck and came down to speak with me. "I am so happy you are here. As soon as I get the ship out of the port, please come up to the bridge."

"Why me?" I asked.

"I have a surprise for you."

"Okay," I said.

The ship pulled away from the dock. The rain was falling hard, the wind was strong and the sea was rough. The deck would tilt left, then right, then forward and back. It was hard to walk. I had to hold tightly to the rail as I climbed up the stairs because the sea threw me first one way, then the other. Down below, the people were sitting on the hard wooden floor, like cattle, but no one was complaining. Everyone was thankful to be getting out of Lebanon.

When I got up to the bridge, the captain took me down a flight of steps to a bedroom that had two sets of bunk beds. "Here," he said, "You are a man of God, sleep here."

"Captain," I asked. "Why me?"

"A year ago," he said, "you were on my ship from Limassol, Cyprus, to Haifa with about five hundred passengers. About one hundred of those passengers were with your tour group. You asked us if we would play a tape recording of one of your messages over the ship's loudspeakers. You were preaching about Jesus, Jesus, Jesus. Everywhere anyone went on the ship, they heard you preach. Some of passengers got angry and complained to my officers, but I told my officers to tell them that if they did not like it they could jump overboard."

We laughed.

He had heard my message. He knew what kind of preacher I was. Now he wanted to give me a room where I could sleep. You can imagine my joy. I sat on the edge of my bunk and tried to put on my pajamas, but the sea was tossing the ship so much that I would aim my foot at my pajama leg, then miss the opening as the ship lurched in yet another direction. I sat laughing for some time before I got them on.

Then I went to bed. In five minutes, I was sound asleep. The ship rocked me like a mother rocks a baby. I slept for six hours. At three in the morning, I awoke. Someone was moaning. I looked around. There was a man in the next bed moaning as if he were going to die.

"Good morning," I said.

"It is not a good morning," he replied. "It is the worst morning in my life. A few hours ago, we nearly sank."

"Really!" I said. "What was I doing?"

"You were sound asleep."

The man was lying in the bed wearing a beautiful suit. I wondered, *Who is this man?*

"What is your business, sir?" I asked.

"I'm from New York. I am a director for the American Life Insurance Company."

Then, as sick as he was, he asked me, "Do you have life insurance?"

I was still in my pajamas, so he had no idea that I was a pastor. "Oh, yes," I answered. "I have very good life insurance."

"Which company?" he asked.

"The biggest one in the whole world."

"Hmm," he said. "I thought we were the largest company."

"No, my company's bigger than yours."

"Are there representatives in Lebanon?"

"Yes, in every country."

"Where are the headquarters?"

"In the best and securest place." I said. My insurance is sea insurance, air insurance, land insurance—and the director of this insurance company pays for me. I never pay." I waited eagerly for his next question which was, "What's his name?"

"Jesus," I said with a big smile.

"Oh." he said, looking at me like a deflating balloon. I could tell he was disappointed.

"Just a minute," I said. "Tell me somebody more precious than Jesus."

"What is your name?" he said.

"Samuel Doctorian."

"Oh, I've heard about you. Are you the preacher in the Middle East that goes from country to country?"

"Yes, that's me."

"Would you pray for my wife?" he asked. "She is dying of cancer."

So I got up from my bed and laid hands on him and prayed for his wife, and then for him. We had a wonderful time of prayer.

Only heaven can tell what would have happened had I not left Lebanon that night. That cattle boat was the last boat to leave the harbor for many weeks. I believe God sent His angel to get me out of the country. Once again, God was watching out for us!

36

Blacklisted!

For the last two decades, I have not been able to get into Egypt or Syria. I am banned—blacklisted. The Egyptians call me a "Christian revolutionary." I have been thrown out of the country many times.

The first time I went to Egypt, I was only 23 years old and Gamal Abdel Nassar was in power. After I led revival services all over the country, they booted me out of the country. Then Nasser died in 1970 and Anwar el-Sadat became president. Under Sadat, the whole situation changed and I was able to go back to Egypt. I had even greater meetings than before.

Then in 1981, Muslim extremists jumped out of a truck during a parade and shot Sadat with a machine gun. After Sadat was assassinated, the Muslin Brotherhood, a radical Islamic group, threatened to kill me, so the Egyptians put me out of the country again.

Then Mubarak became president, security loosened up a bit, and I could get in once more. I had tremendous meetings until one afternoon when the police came to the place where I was staying and insisted that I go with them. I was on my way to the meeting, but they would not let me go. They took me to police headquarters, and kept me there all night. In the morning, officers escorted me to the airport, and put me on a plane to Cyprus. Since then I have not been able to get into Egypt.

Five years ago, I tried to sneak into Egypt with a Brazilian tour group. I hoped they would be my cover. I was traveling with the president of the Presbyterian Churches of Brazil, Pastor Guilermino. We had almost made it through immigration. I had a new American passport, so I thought that maybe they would not recognize me. They had stamped an Egyptian visa in my passport, and I was thinking, *I am going to make it!* My luggage had already gone through customs, and all the rest of the tour group had made it through, except me and Pastor Guilermino. But then they took my passport and entered my name into their computer. Suddenly, a red light began to flash, a buzzer sounded, and the doors swung shut. Immediately, they came, took my passport, and pulled me back inside.

Praise God, Pastor Guilermino was still with me, and he stayed by my side for six hours, until two o'clock in the morning. The Egyptians would not let me enter the country. At two A.M., I said to Guilermino, "Go to the hotel. Join your flock. When you get there, send my luggage back."

I was seventy years old, but they made me sit in a chair until two in the morning—after a long flight from Brazil. I asked them if I could sleep at the airport hotel, but they said, "Only with written permission from the authorities." I said, "Okay, get it." By four o'clock, they got the permit saying that I could sleep at the hotel inside the airport. They charged me three hundred dollars for those few hours.

Two officers took me to my room, and then they expected me to tip them! I said, "You are torturing me, and you want money! I am sorry. Good night!" I closed the door.

I slept like a baby. By eight o'clock, I had my shower, and was ready. The same two officers came to escort me to a flight to Tel Aviv that was leaving at 10 o'clock. They charged me two or three times the normal fare, and insisted on cash, not credit.

The two officers walked me to the plane. To make them happy and leave a Christian testimony, I gave them 20 dollars each. That is a lot of money in Egypt. They were thrilled. They wanted a tip earlier; they got it now. At the steps to the plane; they gave me my passport.

I was going up the steps when I remembered something! I came back down. I am sure they wondered, *Why is he coming back?*

I said, "Jesus said, when a country does not receive you, shake the dust from your feet." In front of them, I shook my feet on the ground, then walked up the steps and on to the plane to fly to Tel Aviv. Since that time, I have not been back to Egypt.

* * *

The Syrians hate me even more than the Egyptians. I think that if the Syrian government could get their hands on me they would kill me. They have put me on their blacklist as a "dangerous, notorious person." Imagine. Little me. Dangerous. Notorious.

Today it is impossible for missionaries to get into Syria. The country is closed to anyone who wants to preach the Gospel. Even though I am not supposed to get in, every once and a while I sneak back in. I pray that they will not recognize my name. I cross the border, encourage the brethren, and then before the authorities know I am there, I get out.

One time they caught me. I was trying to enter Syria from Iraq, up near the northern end of both countries. I was driving a car with my father-in-law and my brother-in-law. We had driven that day from Mosul, the old city of Nineveh, in Iraq. I wanted to go to Aleppo, Syria, to preach, then drive south to our home in Lebanon.

They caught me at the border. I had pulled up in front of the immigration office and my brother-in-law and I had gone inside. My father-in-law was waiting outside in the car.

Inside, the Syrian official took my passport and made me sit down, across a table from him. I glanced up. Two soldiers with guns were watching me. The Syrian officer looked inside my passport. He must have recognized my name because he told my brother-in-law, "You go. He is staying here."

My brother-in-law said to me in Armenian, "What should we do?"

Thankfully, Syrians don't understand a word of Armenian. We can speak and they don't understand what we are saying, but when they speak Arabic we understand every word.

"Listen carefully," I said to my brother-in-law in Armenian. "Go out and turn the car around, facing Iraq."

"What are you going to do?" he asked.

"I am going to come out and drive us back to Iraq."

"They will shoot you!"

"Just do what I am telling you," I implored. "Turn the car around."

My brother-in-law left. I eyed the officer across the table. I looked up at the two soldiers with their submachine guns. I began to pray, "Dear Lord, bind them. Bind them." I boldly got up, reached across the table, and took my passport out of the hands of the officer seated across from me. No one moved or said a word. They were watching me with a fixed gaze, but they were bound. They were frozen. They were completely under the power of God. I walked out and dashed to the car. I hit the gas and drove as fast as I could back toward Iraq.

Then I remembered. Back down the road there was a gate—a metal bar across the road, guarded by a soldier. How would we get past the gate? As we approached the gate, I saw that it was open and no one was there. How it happened, I do not know. Someday, heaven will tell us. We drove right through the no-man's land between the two countries, six kilometers, to the Iraqi border.

At the border we begged the guard to let us enter Iraq again. The soldier said, "Three hours ago, you crossed through here. Why are you coming back?" The whole time we had been driving, we had worried that the Syrians would call the border and stop us, but this guard seemed to know nothing about our narrow escape.

I couldn't tell them that the Syrians would not let me in. I would be in trouble right there.

"I don't like the roads in Syria," I said, "they are terrible."

The guard laughed. I knew that the Lord had given me wisdom.

"Your visa was for one entrance," he said sternly. "You've used it. Now you have no visa."

"Come on," I said, in a friendly tone. "You can give me a visa. I am so tired and weary."

"Well," he hesitated. "How long will you stay?"

"Just one day." I was planning to drive south through Iraq and cross the border into Jordan. Syria surrounds Lebanon on three sides, but from Jordan, I could get a flight to Beirut. My father-in-law and my brother-in-law could drive the car back to Lebanon though the southern part of Syria. They would be safe if I was not with them.

Thank God, the Iraqi border guard stamped our passports. I had no idea how long the Syrian soldiers would stay bound, but they were bound long enough for us to escape!

I drove back to Mosul. We got to the hotel about 10 o'clock at night. When we got to our room my father-in-law began to shake from head to toe. He began crying and said, "The Lord delivered me from the sword of the Turks when I was a little boy, but today I thought we were going to be killed by the Syrians."

At his words, I too began to tremble. Until then I had stayed remarkably calm, but in the privacy of our hotel room, I thought back at what had transpired, and my whole body shook. Normally my father-in-law and brother-in-law share a room and I get another room, but my father-in-law insisted that I stay with them that night. He was afraid that even inside Iraq, they would come in the night and kill me.

The next morning we drove to Jordan. I planned to fly from Amman to Beirut, but in the early morning hours, while I was still lying in bed, the Lord gave me a vision. In the vision, I was in the car. I came to the southern border of Syria. I stopped the car. My brother-in-law got out and walked up to the immigration office, but before he got to the door, the officer came out, glanced at our passports, saw that we were Lebanese and waved us on.

I told my father-in-law, "I'm going through Syria with you."

"No!" he shouted.

"I've seen a vision!" I said. "A vision from the Lord."

He couldn't argue with that. We drove to the Syrian border. I stayed behind the wheel, while my brother-in-law took the passports and walked toward the office. I glanced at my father-in-law. He was praying hard.

"Just watch," I said.

Suddenly the officer stepped out of the office. Before my brother-in-law had even walked up the steps, the officer glanced at our Lebanese passports, and said, "Go on. Welcome to Syria."

My brother-in-law sprinted for the car. "Don't run!" I called to him in Armenian. I was afraid the officer might get suspicious. "Walk normally!"

My brother-in-law slowed to a walk. As soon as he got into the car we crossed the border into Syria. Once we were inside, I said to my father-in-law, "Now that we are here, let's go to Aleppo!" This was three hundred miles out of our way, but I still wanted to go to the brethren and encourage them.

"Never!" he shouted. "Drive straight back to Lebanon. Get out of this country." I had to obey him.

In the midst of all these hard times God gave us a way of escape. He is blessing us in the midst of the impossible. He is a God of miracles. To God be the glory.

* * *

During the war in Beirut both the Syrians and the Israelis invaded the country. At the height of the fighting there were 13,000 Syrian soldiers in Lebanon. Lebanon is a tiny country only 50 miles wide and 120 miles long!

One day when I was at our mission at Peniel, one of our pastors came to me saying, "The Syrians have put up a checkpoint on the road below the mission, between us and the city. Just now, I ran into it coming up the mountain. You have to stop every time you go through and show your papers, your identity card."

I got my binoculars and looked. The Syrians had made their headquarters down in a valley below our mission. I could see their artillery guns, tanks and tents. "Lord," I said, "I wonder if those Syrians know I am here?"

"Praise the Lord," I said. "I think I will go for a little drive." I drove my car up to the checkpoint. They stopped me, of course. The Syrian soldiers were holding big Russian guns.

"Come out," they ordered. I came out. The soldiers searched me to see if I had any weapons. I never carried weapons—except the Bible. The Bible is a double-barreled gun. If the Old Testament misses them, the New Testament will get them. Why should I carry weapons? I have the best weapon: the Word of God.

The soldier looked in my car, and opened the hood and the trunk. No guns. He looked at me. "You can go now. Thank you."

As I drove away, I had an idea. I rushed to the Bible Society and bought hundreds of gospels—Matthew, Mark, Luke and John in Arabic. *This*, I thought, *is the best ammunition there is!* I put them beside me on the seat. I made sure there was a good supply every time that I went through that checkpoint. Sometimes I went to the checkpoint for no reason—just to be checked.

Every time they would say to me, "What's that?"

"The Word of God."

"Can I have one?"

"With joy!"

"Can I have some for my colleagues over there? The ones with the guns?"

"Of course!" I would get out of the car and hand the gospels out to all the soldiers. *Lord*, I would say, *I cannot go to Syria, but the Syrians have come to me!*

The Lord is never defeated.

37

$\mathcal{B}i\mathit{ble}\;\mathcal{L}an\partial\;\mathcal{T}our\mathit{s}$

In 1970, the Lord led me to start taking people on tours of the Bible lands. For years, I had seen thousands of tourists coming to Jerusalem from all over the world. I felt burdened that they traveled such a great distance and never once got to meet their fellow believers in the Middle East. They never attended a single church service. They would go from one to site to another, with their official guides, without knowing that there were fellow believers in the Bible lands.

The Lord led me to organize tours that would bring God's children to the Bible lands. I would guide them, with the Bible in my hand, taking them from country to country, not only showing them the historical and traditional sites, but also organizing Christian religious services for them to attend in Jerusalem, Cairo, Amman, and Beirut.

In the last few years, I have been able to guide hundreds of believers. Many times Christian families brought their unsaved children on the trips, and those children were saved and returned to their home countries transformed by the power of God.

One time we were in Capernaum, near the Sea of Galilee. A young man from Wisconsin, named John, was with our tour group. The day before our tour left America, he had been beaten by a gang. His nose was broken and his face was badly injured. His face was bandaged and his doctors did not think he should go on the trip, but he insisted on getting on the plane.

By the time we got to our first stop in Europe, he was very ill. We continued on to Beirut and took him straight to the hospital, but no doctor would touch his face. They said it was too risky. His face began to swell. He eyes were almost swollen shut. Though it was difficult, we took him with us to Jerusalem, and then to a specialist in Galilee. This doctor also refused to touch him, saying again that it was too risky to try and remove the bandages from his nose. The doctor was afraid that John would hemorrhage. Finally, John decided that he was too ill to continue the trip and that he had better fly back to the United States.

I was preaching that day in the old synagogue in Capernaum. I was standing on a flat rock, with my tour group gathered around me. As often happened, when I start to preach, the other groups leave their guides and join our group, as I proclaim the Word of the Lord. That day the Spirit of the Lord came upon me, and John came forward so that we could lay hands on him and pray for him. We asked God to touch and heal him.

The message that day was about the centurion, who had said to Jesus, "Say the word, Lord, and my servant shall be healed." We prayed, "Lord, touch John." As I laid my hands on John, I could feel the power of God going through his body and instantly, in front of hundreds of people, John was healed. With great courage and boldness, I carefully pealed off his bandages and gently pulled out the cotton that was packed up inside his nose. There were a few drops of blood, but no more than that. John was healed perfectly! The swelling went down before our eyes. He opened his eyes and cried with joy. Everyone was praising the Lord for what He had done!

John's fiancée was so touched by what had happened, that she gave her heart to the Lord. She asked if I would baptize her in the River Jordan. We had a wonderful baptismal service. About seventy people were baptized in addition to John's fiancée.

38

Healing Touch

In my services, I often pray for the sick. I do not make a show of healing, but when I feel the healing presence of the Lord, I will ask those who need a touch of the Master to come forward. I anoint them with oil and commit them into the hand of the Lord. "Let the Master touch you," I urge them. The Lord has healed all kinds of diseases including cancer and AIDS, all over the Middle East, Europe, North and South America, Australia, Africa and Asia.

I love to lay hands on people and see them healed but I love it even more when God heals someone without my even touching them, because then God gets all the glory!

I will never forget our Bible Land Mission Conference that was held in a Catholic monastery called Highlands in the city of Scheveningen in the Netherlands. It was in August of 1977. We had about 1200 people in the cathedral for the Saturday morning service. A man was in the congregation who had been a faithful supporter for years, Brother Bill Boynton. He had often had allergic reactions to food—and he was having a terrible reaction at the conference. He had welts on his body. His eyes were swollen. His lips were swollen, and he was in terrible pain. That morning I went to his hotel room to see how he was, and he told me, "Brother Samuel, I would love to continue the trip with you, but I am miserable. I can never go like this." They had planned to join our tour to Lebanon, Egypt, Armenia and Russia after the conference. Now he looked me in the eye and said, "We can't come. My family and I are flying straight back to Texas."

"If you can wait until after the morning service, I can arrange your return ticket," I told them. "Let's pray now that the Lord will give you peace during these next few hours and then, after the service, we will make the arrangements." During the service, I noticed that Bill, his wife, Louise, and their youngest daughter, Patricia, were sitting about half way back.

That morning the Lord led me to pray that He would touch the sick. Many were healed that morning, including Brother Bill Boynton. He described how, like a flash of light, God cleansed him from the bottom of his feet to the top of his head. He knew instantly that he was healed. He came up to me after the meeting, and with tears rolling down his cheeks, he said, "Brother Samuel, the Lord healed me." He was completely restored, and has not suffered from allergies since.

His daughter, Patricia, was so touched by what Jesus did for her daddy that a week later, while we were on tour, she gave her life to the Lord in the Garden of Gethsemane.

When we got to Moscow we stayed in the Hotel Russia. It is a huge hotel with over two thousand rooms, but they did not have one room where they would let our group gather. It was forbidden for a group larger than five or six people to meet. So we crammed into my hotel room. The whole tour group was there, sitting on the dressers, the bed and the floor.

The Russians warned me that the room was bugged. "Marvelous!" I said. "Let them listen in!" Brother Billy Boynton shared with the group how the Lord healed him. He had eaten everything on the trip and was fine—no allergic reactions. He had not taken any medicine either. The Lord totally had healed him. I hope the Russians heard all of it. Glory to God!

* * *

In 1992, I was preaching at a convention along the west coast of Australia. During the service, the Lord touched many people. I prayed for over one hundred people, anointing each one with oil. The Lord was doing many miracles, but one notable miracle made my heart especially glad.

A woman wearing metal braces on her legs suddenly cried out, "Oh, I feel a marvelous touch." Everybody turned to look at her, wondering, *What's going on?* I hadn't prayed for her. I hadn't laid hands on her. I hadn't gone near her, but suddenly she threw her crutches aside and began to rip the metal braces off her legs. Some people wondered, *Is she losing her mind?* She was so excited. She loosened her metal braces and threw them down. She started walking. When she realized she could walk without crutches, she started running! Hallelujah! She was 46 years old and had been crippled for years.

We were all cheering and praising God. She was healed perfectly.

Some said, "Well, let's wait and see how she is tomorrow. It could be psychological." Part of me started to agree with them. Then I thought, *Oh Lord, you can do it. Lord, I believe, help my unbelief!*

The next day, she came to the convention the next day, beautifully dressed and walking without crutches or any kind of support. She hugged me, praising the Lord. I was especially glad that nobody had prayed for her. Nobody laid hands on her. Nobody anointed her. All the glory goes to Jesus. The touch came from the Divine One. I believe that in the presence of the Lord there is a divine touch.

* * *

Today we need that touch. Many have experienced a touch from God at some point in their lifetime and they know what it means to be touched by God, but many of us need a fresh touch today and some need a shaking. They need renewal in their hearts—a new dedication, a new consecration on the altar. Ask God to touch you today. Let Him revive you, restore you, and renew you.

39

Ireland

While I was a student in Scotland, I crossed the Irish Sea to Northern Ireland many times. On one of those trips, I traveled south to Dublin, the capital of Ireland. I am sure most of you know that Northern Ireland is mostly Protestant and is part of Great Britain, but the country of Ireland, to the south and west, is an independent country and is almost entirely Catholic. There are very few evangelical churches.

When we got to Dublin, I stood on O'Connel Street, the widest street in Europe, on the bridge over the lovely River Liffey. As I looked over the city, the Holy Ghost brought a burden on me. I began to weep. I said, "Oh God, bring me back to Dublin one day. Use me in this great country. In Jesus' Name."

Years passed, and I did return to Ireland. I preached to about two thousand people in Ulster Hall in Belfast, Northern Ireland, a city where the Catholics and the Protestants are constantly fighting. The Holy Ghost was moving mightily in that city. One day, I drove from Belfast to Dublin for the day with Dr. George Frame, the superintendent of the Nazarene Churches in Ireland. He had been the principal of my seminary in Scotland.

While we were there, we had dinner with a man named James Hogan, who had been praying for revival in Dublin for many years.

Hogan was a businessman who owned firm that installed central heating systems in all of the biggest hotels in the city. He was also a Spirit-filled brother. During dinner, he said to me, "I believe you're the man God is going to use to bring revival to Dublin."

I began to cry. I said, "Thank you, Lord. Revival is coming."

That night we drove back to Belfast. The next night, we took an offering. The congregation from Northern Ireland gave money for revival in Dublin. We left the money with Dr. Frame. Plans were made, and I went to Dublin. In Dublin, the man who led the meetings was a blind minister, a Welshman by the name of Glen Thomas. He was full of the Holy Ghost.

That precious blind brother was a mighty prophet of God. He would spend all night on his knees in prayer. He would pray that revival would continue in Dublin. He even made the people pray one night each week. Friday night we would gather together, at about 10 or 11 at night, and pray until six in the morning. We would all be praying and weeping before God. The tremendous presence of God would fall on us.

After one week of meetings, I knew we had to continue. I canceled all of my speaking engagements for the next few weeks. I went to the telegram office in Dublin one night at 11 o'clock and wrote on the telegram form: "Dublin on fire." I handed the sheet of paper to the young man behind the counter. He read it and asked, "Where?"

I had to explain that the fire was burning in our hearts.

After another week, revival spilled out into the streets. I stood on O'Connel Street and began to preach. Hundreds of people gathered round. The traffic stopped. The chief of police came and stood looking at me. I could tell he was wondering, *Who is this man who is holding up traffic?* In my black suit and clerical collar, I think he must have thought I was a Catholic priest, but I wasn't acting like one. As soon as I saw him, I began saying, "What a lovely city! What a marvelous country! Here we have freedom to preach the gospel!"

I told them how the Turks killed my people. The chief of police looked at me and winked as if to say, "Keep preaching!" The police began to divert the traffic around the crowd, and I continued. The Lord was moving in Dublin in a marvelous way.

By the grace of God, I stayed in Dublin four weeks. Night after night, hundreds came to the Lord. That fire is still burning today and I still go to Dublin as often I can. Some of those who were saved at that time are in the ministry and in the mission field today because of the revival in that Catholic country. To God be the glory!

* * *

I have never known a true revival without persecution. I have been persecuted. I have been attacked. I have been accused of many things that never happened. Satan tried to spread rumors about me that would hinder God's ministry. That always happens.

In Ireland, my chief enemies were evangelical leaders who could not understand this strange Armenian preacher from Jerusalem. God was using me, but they could not believe it, and they were jealous. They were my number one enemies. Isn't that a shame? But isn't it marvelous what Jesus says? When they do hateful things against you, you should rejoice! "Rejoice and be exceedingly glad, for great is your reward in heaven, for so they persecuted the prophets who were before you" (Matthew 5:12 NKJV). I was not bitter in my heart against those who attacked me, and I prayed for them. Otherwise, God could not have used me.

40

My Healing

In 1973, while I was in Northern Ireland, I had a heart attack. I was only 43 years old, but I was weighed down with many burdens. The political situation in Lebanon was deteriorating and, of course, eventually led to civil war. There were burdens I carried for our ministry. I had a hundred orphans and three churches that depended on me for support. I was run down. After the heart attack, the doctor said I needed to slow down and take medication or I would need surgery, but I felt I could not stop the work of the Lord. I had to keep going, and the pressure increased.

Two months later, I had a second heart attack—this time in Texas. The X-ray showed that one of my arteries was blocked. It was dangerous, because that part of my heart would die if it did not get enough blood. I felt terrible when I heard the news. I wept before the Lord, praying earnestly. I wanted to slow down, but the work was pressing on me in such a way that I felt I could not.

The doctors insisted that I needed to have heart surgery. I had no medical insurance, and back then that kind of operation would cost over $10,000. I did not want the operation and I did not have the money, but precious brothers and sisters, who loved the ministry and who had been blessed through it, put the money aside and said, "You must have the operation."

The doctors in North Carolina set the date for the surgery. Meanwhile, I had to lead a tour group in Israel. In the Garden of Gethsemane, in the Church of All Nations, I wept before the Lord. I asked Him for a miracle. I felt God touching me. The healing power of Christ, the Great Physician, my Savior, touched me with fire. I felt it go through my whole body, and I knew I was perfectly whole. I rejoiced that the Lord had healed me.

My son, Paul, and my daughter, Jasmine, were kneeling right behind me. At first I did not know they were there, but then I turned and saw them weeping and praying. "Children," I said, "Jesus just healed me. Right now."

We all began to cry. We hugged each other. Then we told the people who were kneeling around the altar that God had healed me. Everyone stood and began praising God, thanking Him for what He had done. Some, of course, doubted. Some thought it was only my emotions. They kept saying that I should be examined again by the doctors.

I knew I was healed, but because my loved ones were so insistent, I went to the doctors. The doctors kept me in the hospital for three days while they did tests. After three days, they came to me and said, "You have been healed perfectly. Your heart is perfect. Your arteries are clear. Even though the old X-rays showed a blockage, now it is gone, so you do not need surgery anymore."

"Doctors," I said, "I know that Jesus healed me in Gethsemane."

They said, "We believe in divine power. Only the Divine One could have done this."

While the doctors were doing their test, I had called my friend John Crouch, in Scotland, to ask him to go to London to cover the meetings where I was scheduled to preach. As soon as the doctor said I had a perfect heart, I quickly took a shower, got dressed, and went to the airport in Charlotte, North Carolina. I called the doctor from the airport. "Where are you?" he asked.

"I am on my way to London."

"But Samuel," he scolded, "you need to recuperate for a few days after all these tests!"

"But you said I had a perfect heart," I answered. "So I am going!"

I arrived in London where John and I held the meetings together. Since that time my heart has been perfect.

Praise and glory to the Lord Jesus Christ!

*　*　*

All my life I have preached about the certainty of death. Death is a reality. There is an angel of death. There is an appointed time. There is a day, an hour, a moment that suddenly your heart will stop. Your blood will stop circulating. Your lungs will stop breathing. Your whole being will be silent.

Now that I am getting older, many people are concerned about my health, my heart, and my blood pressure. They feel I am doing too much. It is true that I get invitations from all over the world, and travel almost all the time. There are so many demands on my time that I am not able to say "No."

More and more I am realizing that death can come to me at any time. I am closer now to death than anything else, but you know what? It is great to be prepared to die. I am serious. I am prepared to go any time. The Bible says PREPARE TO MEET THY GOD. Jesus prepared Himself, so we also should prepare to meet our Creator.

41

Swiss Psychiatrist

On one occasion when I was preaching in the Temple of Montreux near Lausanne, Switzerland, a man came up and asked if he could speak with me privately. I had noticed him because he had such a grave demeanor that he stood out in the crowd.

I studied him. He was well dressed, but so serious.

"Yes, of course," I said keeping my face as serious as his.

"Can you come to my hotel?" he asked.

"Which hotel?"

"The Grand Hotel on the shore of Lake Lausanne."

"Very good," I answered. "I am staying in the same hotel." I was not there because I was rich; I was there because a few days earlier, I had prayed with the owner of the hotel who was sick in the hospital. The Lord touched him. He insisted that I take the best room in the hotel as his guest. Sometimes the Lord spoils me.

"What room are you in?" I asked.

He gave me his room number and said, "Ten o'clock. Good night." The entire conversation was conducted without a smile. He was a very serious man.

Some of the brethren who had seen me speaking with him said, "Do you know who that man is?"

I replied, "No."

"He's a professor at the University of Basel and one of the top psychiatrists in Switzerland."

For a moment, I wondered, *Why does a psychiatrist want to speak with me? Does he think there is something wrong with me?*

There are clocks everywhere in Switzerland, so you had better be on time. At 10 o'clock sharp, I knocked on his door. The professor opened the door, serious as ever.

"Good morning."

"Good morning." I replied as I walked into his room. He motioned to a seat and I sat opposite him.

He began to speak. "I am a psychiatrist."

"I've heard about you. Some people at the meetings recognized you."

"I'm from the University of Basel. I teach there. I have a confession to make."

I thought, *That's lovely. A psychiatrist making a confession!*

"I've tried to help many people, but I need help myself. Can you help me?"

I looked him in the eye. "Doctor, I'm sorry, but I cannot help you."

He looked shocked. "What do you mean? I've heard you preach the last three nights."

"You've come to the wrong person, but the One that helped me can help you."

"Who is He?"

"His name is Jesus."

"I don't believe in Him!"

"Then you're hopeless. You know why? He is the only Savior. You will never find another one."

I began to tell this dear psychiatrist the words of Jesus, one verse after another. ". . the one who comes to Me I will by no means cast out" (John 6:37 NKJV). "Most assuredly, I say to you, he who believes in Me has everlasting life" (John 6:47 NKJV). "If we confess our sins, He is faithful and just to forgive us our sins and to cleanse us from all unrighteousness" (1 John 1:9 NKJV). I quoted verse after verse.

That dear doctor's hands began to tremble. He looked at me and asked, "Why am I trembling?"

"I don't know," I replied. "I am not a psychiatrist."

I paused, then an explanation came to me. "I know something that is not from psychology. It is from the Bible. As soon as your soul heard the Words of Life, it got so excited, your conscience so happy, your spirit so joyful that they trembled. They are hungry for the eternal truth. Your inner being wants to cry out to the Lord Jesus. The moment you say, 'I am going to cry to the Lord,' your conscience will get excited.

"Your soul knows that it will be tortured in hell if you are not saved—if you're not born-again. Your soul knows that it will never enter the kingdom of God. That means your soul and your spirit are lost forever. Oh, that precious, precious soul yearns to be born-again: The very thought makes your body so happy that it trembles."

That explanation had never occurred to me before, but after I said it, I thought, *That's right!*

The dear doctor began to weep. He said, "When I buried my mother four years ago, I didn't shed a tear. I don't remember the last time I cried. It has been many years. I have no feelings and I never cry. But now I am weeping. Why?"

"Doctor," I answered. "I believe the Lord is going to change your life. Let's get on our knees." I got on my knees but the dear doctor remained seated. I wish you could have seen him. He couldn't get down on his knees. It was a battle for him to bow his knees to anyone else, but after a few moments, he managed to get down on his knees.

"Come on," I urged, "call upon the name of the Lord. Say, Lord Jesus." I waited five minutes, seven minutes, but he could not do it. I put my hand on his shoulder. "Lord, release him, loosen him," I prayed. "Let his lips, Lord, be loosened. Let him call on Your name."

Suddenly, he began to say, "Lord Jesus, I never believed in You, but I need help. Help me!" As soon as he said the words heaven came down. He was set free. He turned to me, still on his knees, with tears rolling down his cheeks, and for the first time, he smiled. He put his arms around me and he said, "It is so easy. I've made it so difficult. I feel so good."

His burden had rolled away! It was gone! When we got up, I was so happy. I opened the door to leave, and who was outside? His believing wife! She had been praying for her husband for years. Hallelujah!

She couldn't hear from outside, but she had been there, right outside the door, the whole time praying and wondering what was going on. She didn't want to disturb us, so she didn't open the door. When I opened the door, there she stood, crying. The husband and wife fell on each other, and she cried, "This is the happiest day in my life! My husband found Jesus this morning."

Oh, brothers and sisters, this is why Jesus came! This is the reason. This is why we worship the Lord, so souls can be born-again. Jesus came into the world to save sinners.

42

My Manager, the Holy Spirit

The Holy Spirit is my manager. I go where He tells me to go. He knows what will happen and why I need to be exactly where I am. Once I was in Amsterdam scheduled to fly to Chicago via Zurich on Swiss air. I was so tired, I thought, *Why go to Zurich and change flights to go to Chicago? Let me find out if there is a KLM flight that will take me directly to Chicago.*

I went to the KLM lady and I gave her a big smile. You smile; they smile back. You don't smile; they don't smile back. She smiled back. I said to her, "I've got a ticket here, Swiss Air to Zurich then Chicago, but I want to go directly. Do you have a direct flight?" In two hours' time there was a flight.

I said, "Try to book me." I am a member of KLM Club. I gave my number, and she found my name.

She said, "I've got a seat for you."

"Can you do me another favor?" I asked. "I am so tired. If it is not full, can you give me three seats together? Just block the other seats and don't give them to any one else?" I wanted to take my shoes off and stretch out so I could relax during the eight-hour flight.

She said, "I think I can. The plane is not full."

When I got on the plane I was so happy. I quickly put things on the other seats so no one would change seats and sit beside me. I wanted to be by myself. I slipped my shoes off, leaned back and relaxed. In a few minutes, the plane took off. I was content. I had my reading material and Bible beside me. I had a few notebooks out. Now, I thought, I can just eat and drink and sleep and pray—and that's it.

When the pilot turned off the fasten seat belt sign, I loosened my seat belt and got ready to stretch out.

"Are you Samuel Doctorian?"

I looked up. *Oh Lord! Where did he come from?*

"Yes, that's me," I answered wearily. "Samuel Doctorian."

"Do you remember me?"

I did not know what to say.

"Eighteen years ago . . ."

Oh Lord, I really don't know, I prayed and asked him, "Are you Egyptian?"

"You remember! When I was 12 years old, you came to our home in Naggi Hammadi, between Asyut and Luxor. I was paralyzed. I couldn't walk. You anointed me with oil, and the Lord touched me and healed me perfectly."

It all came back. "Of course, I remember you. I remember the day we prayed for you. What's has happened? Where are you going?"

He looked a little sad, then said, "I am married now. My wife and I have three children. We were living in Libya. I was working as an accountant in a bank. We had a lovely house and a beautiful car. For the sake of my children, I gathered some neighbor children and taught them from the Bible. We had a little Sunday school in my home. The authorities heard about it. The seized all our possessions—my bank account and car—and gave us 24 hours to get out of the country. We could only take one suitcase each. They threw us out. We had to leave everything and fly back to Cairo. Please," he said, "pray for me."

"I will do it right now," I replied. "Where are you going?"

"San Francisco."

"You are going to look for work as an accountant in a bank?"

"That's it."

"Give me your hand." I began to pray. I have a loud voice. I can't pray quietly. People all around me heard me pray. "Lord, you know he has lost everything for Your name's sake. Find a job in a bank for him. Thank you, Lord, for the answer. In Jesus' name."

When I finished praying, the man behind us said, "Excuse me, Reverend. I heard every word. Can I help this young man?"

"How can you help him?" I asked.

"I am the president of Bank of America in Chicago. My best friend is president of the bank in San Francisco. We'll get a job for this young man."

The young man began to cry. He hugged me.

You see before the plane even landed, the Lord answered the prayer. He got the job. He brought his wife and children to America. They are living in San Francisco now, having a marvelous time. To God be the glory!

Who changed my thoughts and desires, so that I flew from Amsterdam and not Zurich? Who put me on that plane? Of course, the Lord. These things are miraculous interventions of God. Even now as you read this book, it is all in the will of God.

A few minutes later, the chief steward came to speak with me. He had overheard everything. He had been in the galley, just one row up from my seat, while we were talking. He asked, "I am sorry, Reverend, I couldn't help but hear. Is it true? Was he paralyzed and you prayed for him and he was healed?" I said, with a grin, "Don't ask me, ask him. It happened to him." I could tell that the steward was very touched by the story.

* * *

When you have the Holy Ghost inside you He speaks to you. Once I took a short trip on a Turkish ship. That in itself is a miracle for an Armenian, because the Turks and Armenians are enemies. The Swiss brethren had said to me, "Samuel, why don't you relax for two or three days? You can change your clothing so no one will know that you're a minister of God and take it easy. You're so tired."

I said, "Okay." I was weary. The brethren bought me a first class ticket on a ship. They bought me a blue suit and a tie. When I put it on, I felt 10 years younger. I got on the ship and went to my first class cabin, where I dropped off my luggage and then went to the dining room.

I was alone, so the maitre d' led me to a table by myself. I had been there a few minutes, when I saw another man coming. He was smiling at everyone, greeting them, "Good evening, good evening." They led him to my table and he sat down.

The moment he sat down the Holy Spirit began to speak to me.

"Welcome, Sweden," I said.

"That's right," he said. "Do you know me?"

"No," I said. "I've never met you before." I waited a bit then said, "You're a professor of psychology."

"That's right. Have you heard of me?"

"No. Never. I haven't heard of you." I looked at him and said, "You're a miserable man."

His eyebrows shot up, and he looked a little shocked. "What makes you say that? Didn't you see me walk though the dining room? I was smiling at *everybody*."

"That is all put on. You've never known real joy. Every week you fly to Finland for two days, you teach at the university. Then you fly back home. You're miserable."

"Let me ask you," he said angrily. "How you know this?"

"Just a minute," I said. At that moment, God was telling me more. "You've just divorced your fourth wife." *Married four times*, I thought. *He must be miserable.*

"Excuse me," he said. "Why are you reading my mind?

I did not answer.

Then he asked, "What is your profession?"

"What do you think?" I asked.

He said, "At first I thought that you were an ambassador to some country."

It is the suit, I thought.

"Later, I thought, you're a businessman," he continued.

That's my nose, I thought. Then I said. "No. I am neither. I am a servant of God. A preacher of the gospel."

"You mean a pastor?" he asked.

"Something like that."

"I hate pastors. If I had known you were a pastor, I would not have sat at this table." Then he said, "But I think I like you."

"Thank you sir," I replied. Then I asked, "Where are you going?"

"To Cairo, Egypt, to play golf."

As soon as I asked the question, God whispered the answer. "No," I said, shaking my head. "You are making plans for the fifth marriage. The girl is flying over to meet you."

He looked at me with his mouth hanging open.

I didn't know these things. God did. It was the marvelous Holy Ghost telling me about this man. At the end of the meal, we left each other. I knew he was miserable.

The next day I heard a knock on my cabin door. I knew it was him. I opened the door and he came in. He said, "I couldn't sleep last night. Everything you said is true."

You could see that he had been crying. He said, "Three times, I wanted to commit suicide. I've never known real joy in my life. I've just divorced my fourth wife. She was only 24 years old. Our marriage only lasted two years. I am a miserable man."

We fell on our knees, and this is what he said, "I never dreamed that one day I would be kneeling beside a pastor and praying. But I need help."

It was wonderful to pray with him and lead him to the Lord.

43

Tiny Countries, Big Hearts

I get invitations to preach all over the world, but the strangest invitation I ever got was the one from Surinamee. I met a precious brother in Holland who insisted that I come to Surinamee. "Where is Suriname?" I asked. I had never heard of it, so I had to look on a map to find it. Suriname is a small country north of Brazil. It used to be Dutch Guyana but now it is called Suriname.

I prayed about it and God showed me in a vision that I must go. I flew to the capital, Paramaribo. As soon as I walked off the plane, I wanted to turn around and get back on the plane again. It was burning, scorching hot.

I did not know anyone in Suriname, but I knew that two Christian brothers were to meet me. I looked at the crowd and saw two men—one who looked Indian, one who looked Chinese. I thought, *They must be the ones.* The brother who had first told me about Suriname was half white and half black. It is a country that has every ethnic group, every nationality in the whole world in one little country. You can find nearly every nationality except Armenians. I didn't find any Armenians.

Sure enough, when I came up to the two men, they said, "Samuel Doctorian?"

"That's right!" I answered.

I hugged both of them and we went to their car. As we drove to the city, I asked, "What have you got planned for revival meetings?"

"Nothing."

"Have you arranged for a hall?"

"No," they said. "Nobody knows you are coming. Not even our wives."

What's the matter with them? I wondered. *How can we have revival in the time I am here if they have not made any arrangements?*

"Don't worry," they said. "We had to wait until you got here. Now that you are in the country we can start to make arrangements. If we did anything ahead of time, the government may have kept you out. We had some evangelists come a few years ago and there was a scandal, so now the government will not allow preachers and evangelists to enter the country."

I thought, *Well, let's see what happens.*

The two men told their wives that Doctorian had come to Suriname and in no time at all they had a hall that seated three hundred people. That night the hall was filled and the next night the hall could not contain the crowds. The Spirit of God was moving. We moved to a church that seated six hundred, called The Church of God's Trumpet. Soon it was packed.

Once again, I had to cancel my meetings in America and around the world. The Holy Spirit was touching people, and I could not leave. I stayed in Suriname one solid month, preaching daily. The Holy Ghost was moving. The largest church in Paramaribo, the Roman Catholic Cathedral, opened its doors to us. It was a miracle of God.

One night, the Bishop of the Catholic Cathedral called me two hours before the meeting was scheduled to start at 7:00 P.M. "Rev. Doctorian, you might as well come now because the cathedral is so crowded that we can't get another person inside." I had to preach at 5:00 instead of 7:00 in that big cathedral. Night after night, the Holy Spirit saved thousands of people. Glory to God.

There is a price for revival. When I first got to Suriname, the two brothers took me to a very poor hotel. It was blistering hot with no air conditioning. The worst part was that the room was filled with bugs and little creatures. I don't even know their names—geckos or lizards, perhaps, were walking all around the room. It was disgusting. "Lord," I cried, "What have I done that You have brought me here?"

The best thing you can do when you are feeling like that is to fall on your knees before God and cry. That is exactly what I did. I fell on my knees and began to sob. I had a little weeping spell and while I was weeping, the Holy Ghost came on me afresh. He filled me with His glory, in such a way that when I got up and began to wipe my tears, the mosquitoes looked wonderful. The little creatures looked so charming. I said, "Welcome, little friends, to my room!"

That day I experienced the great truth: when revival comes, it starts in you. Don't expect revival to start in somebody else. People often say, "We need revival. We need revival!" I think they should say, "I need revival! I need revival!" When the revival burns in you, others will catch the fire. I needed a touch of God first for myself. And when the Lord visited me, I said, "I will pay any price. I don't care how much I sweat. I don't care how many suits I ruin. I don't care if conditions are terrible. I don't care what they feed me. I won't even ask. I will just eat."

You have to do whatever the Lord says no matter what the conditions. When I was preaching in a poor part of Egypt, every time I went out to preach, my poor wife would ask, "What creatures have you brought home with you tonight?" She stayed home with Paul because he was a tiny baby, but I would unintentionally bring home little bugs and things from the poor people. Those bugs never bothered me. They didn't like me, but they bit my dear wife and my little son, Paul.

Revival has a price. You have got to come down to the level of the people to be a blessing. Suriname is such a poor country that when I go there, I don't expect them to give me money.

In America, they have preachers who teach that if you are dedicated to God, He will make you rich. The Bible never promises that. Those preachers can only teach that God guarantees prosperity to Christians because they are preaching in a rich country like America. I wish they would go and teach that in Suriname; or teach that in Lebanon, where people are hungry for bread. Some of those prosperity preachers become so rich. They have beautiful diamond rings, lizard or alligator shoes, beautiful ties, and a lavish lifestyle.

They can never preach from the verse: "Silver and gold have I none; but such as I have give I thee." (Acts 3:6). What I have, I give. I can preach from that verse.

Once when Naomi and I were in Asyut, a very rich family invited us to their home for dinner. I had led some of the family members to Jesus, and they loved me very much. Their home was a palace. Servants everywhere. We had the most marvelous dinner. While we were eating dinner, the dear mother, said, "We have a lovely room prepared for you. We would love for you and your family to stay here."

I opened my mouth to say "yes," but my wife stopped me. In Armenian, she said, "Don't accept this invitation." It is very convenient that we speak a language that most people don't understand, but at that moment, I could only think, *Naomi! Please! Think of it! We will have our own chauffeur. Our own beautiful car. We will have servants to take care of us. We will stay where ambassadors and royal families have stayed.*

She said, "I will tell you the reason later. Don't accept it!" Well, I had to obey my wife. Even though she is younger than I, sometimes she is wiser. If I did not obey her, I would have had trouble later. I said to our hostess, "We'll think about it. We will let you know later."

When we got home, Naomi said, "Samuel, when you are preaching to such poor people, you can't stay in a rich home. When they hear that you are staying in such a rich home, it will not be a good testimony for your preaching." She was right.

* * *

Once I was in Ouagadougou, Burkina Faso. I was the only white person on the platform. The entire congregation is black, with beautiful white teeth when they smile. The last day I was there, they wanted to give me a love offering. They gave little hand-made musical instruments, and small change: nickels and small pennies. The offering container was so heavy. I wept when I took it. I hadn't realized that they were taking it for me because I don't understand their language. I took that offering and split it among the four pastors that were helping with the meetings. I wouldn't take a penny out of Suriname or Burkina Faso. I felt I was there to give.

There is a price to pay for revival.

*   *   *

In the end, the rich lady in Asyut, the one who owned the palatial home, gave me the key to her home and command of her servants so we could use that home for our meetings. We had many wonderful times in that house. Some of the Egyptian brothers said to me, "When we were children, we used to pass by that palace and say, 'Oh I wish we could go in there one day!'" God was so good to us. He gave us that home to use as a revival center for the city. How He blessed us. To God be the glory!

44

My Family

For most of my life I have been on the road far more than I have been home. When we first married, my dear wife, Naomi, traveled with me, but when the children got to be school age, she began to stay home with them. I would often take one or two of our children with me, and at times the whole family, but mostly we were apart. This was very difficult for my family.

Once I had Paul and Jasmine with me when revival broke out in Dublin. Paul was about 12 years old and Jasmine was about 10. I told them, "I have to send you back to Beirut. School is about to start and I need to stay here." It was very difficult to put the two of them on a plane for Beirut, but I had to stay in Dublin and trust that God would care for them.

While we were apart, I would call when I could. My wife and I would make decisions together, on the phone, and then I would talk with each of the children. Now the children are grown, with families of their own and we have mobile phones, so it is easier to call. I call my wife, Naomi, and talk to her often, sometimes every day, and I talk to each of my children every few days.

But even with mobile phones, it is very hard to be apart when you are going through trials. Many people seem surprised to hear that we have trials. They think I am a spiritual giant who does not need their prayers, but we all have our trials. Many people come to me with their needs, and want me to pray for them, and I am happy to pray for them, but my family and I also need prayer.

Back in 1991, we nearly lost our son, Danny. In October of that year, quite suddenly he began to lose weight. In a few short weeks, he dropped from 180 pounds to just 134 pounds. By November he was in the hospital. He had been diagnosed with ulcerative colitis a few years earlier, and now he was having a major flare up. We didn't know what to do. Every day he was getting weaker and weaker. He was losing so much blood. The doctors recommended surgery. They wanted to take out a large section of his intestines, but Danny's wife, Nora, felt that that was not the right decision, and we agreed with her.

I was traveling, calling home every few days to check on my family. One day Naomi called. I could tell she was very upset. "Samuel, Danny is in very serious condition. I think we may lose him." I could hear the distress in her voice. I called Danny's wife, Nora, and she also said, "Daddy, it looks really serious, but I have told the doctors that I don't feel surgery is the answer."

I supported her. I felt she was right.

I desperately wanted to cancel everything and rush home.

I called Danny in the hospital.

"Danny, my son," I asked him, "should I come?"

"Daddy, I don't want to hinder the work of God," he said, "but please pray for me."

I was in the middle of transporting two used cars to Lebanon. The cars were packed with supplies for our mission in Beirut. I didn't know how I could leave them and expect them to arrive intact. They were already loaded on to the cargo ship. My heart ached. I felt I should go with the cars to Beirut, but I wanted to rush home. While I struggled the ship set sail.

In my cabin, I fell to my knees weeping and crying. "Jesus!" I cried. Jesus come into the cabin. He said, "I have touched your son right now and healed him."

I wiped my tears. I looked in the mirror. My eyes were red with crying. I washed my face and went to the officer.

"Officer, I need to call California immediately."

He said, "Our connection is not very good. You won't be able to hear clearly, and it will cost you lots of money." He continued, "Why don't you wait and call tomorrow when we get to Greece?"

I thought, *That is wise.* As soon as we got to Greece, I called the hospital.

Danny answered the phone.

"How are you, Son?" I asked, near tears.

"Daddy, I have been healed. Yesterday I felt the power of God touch me."

I asked, "What was the hour, Son?"

"One o'clock in the morning."

It was the exact hour I had prayed for him.

"Danny, that was exactly the time that Jesus told me that He healed you!"

"Jesus touched me," he cried.

I was overwhelmed with emotion. I left the ship, with the cars and supplies on board, and caught a plane to California.

My son, Paul, picked me up from the airport. We drove straight to the hospital.

We held each other—father, son and mother—all weeping. Over the next few days, Danny began to get stronger. He had been in the hospital for four weeks, but now we got to take him home. Nora and Danny stayed in our home so he could rest and recuperate over the next two weeks. He was perfectly healed—without surgery.

I knew that the devil was attacking my son because of my work, but God is stronger than the devil. The devil is a defeated foe who cannot thwart God's loving power. We are not alone: God will not fail us.

45

Indonesia

The first time I went to Indonesia, God opened the door for me to go in a marvelous way. I planned to go, I prayed to go, but I did not have the money. I told no one, for we are not beggars. When you tell someone what you need, that is not faith. Faith is when you tell people what God has done after the Lord has supplied your need.

So I told no one but God. Then an elderly couple came to me and said, "For years we have been praying for Indonesia and hoping to go there, but we never made it. Will you go for us? We want to pay for your ticket. Please go."

How grateful I was to the Lord for answering my prayer!

While I was in Indonesia, winning hundreds of souls to the Lord, I wrote that dear couple, saying, "You have a part in every soul I am winning in Indonesia."

I love Indonesia. It is a tremendous country with more than 16,500 islands. One of the largest is Java, which has one of the highest population densities in the world—more than two thousand people per square mile! One hundred ten million people live on that one island and the largest city, Jakarta, has about 11 million people.

Indonesia is 90 percent Muslim and can be a dangerous place for Christians. When I minister there I keep a cross in my hand, a big one. I lift it up. The cross is the power of God. No cross, no hope. No cross, no message. No cross, no salvation. No cross, no forgiveness. No cross, no life. The cross is our only salvation.

* * *

Indonesians have heard that I'm a slave of Jesus, so they treat me like one! They pick me up at the airport in Jakarta and take me immediately from the airport to the hotel. I have five minutes to wash my face, grab my Bible, and off we go to the meetings. In Indonesia, I often preach three or four times a day. Once I preached at 29 meetings in only two weeks' time.

I've been all over Indonesia—to Bali, Sulawesi, Java, Toraja, Tentena. I have been all over the island of Sumatra. I thank God that the Gospel is the same throughout the world. I love the Indonesian people. I wish you could see them worship, playing their wonderful tambourines while 10 or 20 young people line up and dance so beautifully.

* * *

The first time I went to Indonesia, I flew into Jakarta. When I got off the plane, I saw a man holding a picture of me. He was the chauffeur for the man who owned the Fuji Film factory in Jakarta. Sunkorno's factory employs eight thousand people. The chauffeur drove me to Sunkorno's home in a beautiful Mercedes. The home was like a palace. I was living in abundance there.

The whole time I was in Jakarta, Sunkorno's chauffeur drove me from meeting to meeting in that Mercedes. It is so hot in Indonesia that during the meetings I would sweat. Then the chauffeur would pick me up, and I could cool off in the nice air-conditioned car.

On one of our tours of the Holy Land, I led Sunkorno, that precious man, to Christ and baptized him in the Jordan River. Hallelujah! It was fantastic.

* * *

In 1992, I was in Surabaya on the island of Java. Surabaya is the second largest city on Java, and when I am there I always preach in an immense church, where they can seat eight thousand people at one service. The church has five floors. You can see the platform from two floors—the ground level and the gallery. From the platform, you can see thousands of people on both floors before you. On the third and fourth floors, the people can't see the preacher, and he can't see them, but the people can watch the service on television monitors.

One day I was preaching on the ministry of the mighty Holy Spirit. I had just finished preaching and had not even started to pray when everyone felt a mighty wind blow through the place. Everyone could hear it. Everyone could feel it. The whole place was on fire. My interpreter, a medical doctor named Dr. Daniel, was standing beside me crying out to God. He turned to me and said, "Samuel, I've been in the church, in ministry, for years, but I have never felt the power of the Holy Ghost so strongly."

I wondered if they felt the wind of the Holy Ghost upstairs, too, so I asked some of the brothers, "How was it up there?"

"OOOHHH," one said. "You should have felt the power that fell: it was tremendous." Another one said, "It was even greater than what they told us was happening down below." I realized that the Holy Ghost had come from above. They had received Him first; we got it later. They were not left out; they got even more of this special blessing than we had down below.

Later that year, I was in the city of Ugun Pundung in Indonesia preaching to a large audience in a great hotel. The place was crowded. There was such a hunger for God. I was preaching from Acts 4, reading verse 31, where it says, "And when they had prayed, the place was shaken where they were assembled together; and they were all filled with the Holy Ghost, and they spake the Word of God with boldness."

I finished preaching. I walked down off the platform. My interpreter walked down with me, and we sat in the front row. I was sitting next to the manager of Continental Airlines Indonesia. He is Chinese and represents our Mission in Indonesia and handles my meetings for me in that great country.

Suddenly, an earthquake shook the building. Then it stopped. Then a second earthquake, shook the building stronger than the first. I thought, *Which way should I run if the building begins to collapse?* It stopped, and a few seconds later the building again shook with another earthquake. Those in the back felt it more than those in the front. Everyone was shaken. Everybody wondered what had happened.

To our amazement—God be the glory—there was no earthquake in the city, it only happened in the church. No one else felt it.

Some who read these words may doubt, but I know it happened to me, and there were hundreds of witnesses. The place was shaken in such a way that everyone began to weep. The presence of God came upon us. He was shaking us.

This is my fervent prayer that the Lord will shake you, too.

* * *

God is doing wonders in Indonesia. In 1993, I got visas to take 154 Indonesians to Israel. This is a miracle. Why? Because Indonesia is the largest Muslim country in the world, and it has no diplomatic relations with Israel. Indonesians are not supposed to go to Israel. The Israeli consulate in Switzerland said to me, "It is fantastic that you are able to bring Indonesians to Israel." We had a marvelous tour of the Holy Land.

46

Resurrection!

Another time, when I was preparing to go to Indonesia, the people who had invited me called to say that they were going to have a banquet to welcome me to the country the day after I got there. Eight hundred people were coming. I was amazed. I told my boys, "Imagine! Eight hundred people are coming to the banquet." One of my boys believed me, but my other son—I won't say which one—said, "Daddy, did you hear right? Did they say eight hundred or 80?"

"I heard right!" I insisted. "They said eight hundred. I know that evangelists tend to exaggerate, but I am not exaggerating! I heard eight hundred."

To prove it, I asked the organizers the next time they called, "Are there eight hundred coming to the banquet or 80?"

"It was eight hundred but now it is one thousand!"

"Very good!" I said, hanging up. I turned to my son, "It is a thousand."

The first night I was in Indonesia the banquet organizers wanted me to meet with two hundred men. They were doctors, lawyers and top businessmen. I was to anoint them with oil so that they would be prepared to minister to those who were coming to the banquet. I wish you could have seen them, all two hundred on their knees as I anointed them. The next night they would minister to people of many faiths—Buddhist, Confucianist, and Muslims—who would be coming to the banquet.

During this preliminary meeting, Doctor Daniel, my interpreter, said to me, "Brother Samuel, see that lady sitting in the back there?" I looked. She was the only lady in the place. "She came tonight because her husband is playing the music synthesizer and she did not want to be left alone. She is brokenhearted. It is so sad. She was expecting their first baby, but they just found out a week ago that the baby is dead! Can you just say a few words of comfort to her? Can you pray that the Lord will comfort her?"

"Yes, I will do that," I said.

I looked at her. She was a lovely lady from a Chinese background. I could see her heart was shattered. I was praying in my heart, *What shall I say, Lord? Give me the right words.* Suddenly the Lord began to say, "Samuel, I am the resurrection and the life. I can raise that baby to life."

I said, *Lord, just a minute. Just a minute. Is this You or me? I don't want to make a mistake. Tomorrow there is a big banquet in my honor.*

"ARE YOU DOUBTING ME?" said the Lord.

No, no! I am not doubting You, Lord.

"Samuel, did you forget what I did last year in South Africa?"

I thought back. Last year I had prayed for a Portuguese couple in South Africa, named Tony and Carla. They had been trying to have a baby for years. I had laid hands on them a year before, and a prophecy had come that she would have a baby. I even saw a vision of the baby in Carla's arms. As I shared the prophecy with her, Carla began to cry.

A few months later, Carla's boss, Vergilio, had called me to tell me, "Pastor, Carla is expecting a baby."

I was thrilled.

Nine months later, I was back in Johannesburg. Carla was leading worship at a banquet on Saturday morning for the Portuguese business community in South Africa. She was noticeably pregnant and leading the singing with great enthusiasm. She was jumping, she was shouting. I said to myself, *Calm down Carla. You are expecting a baby. Don't jump like that!* I didn't say it out loud, but I thought it.

That night Vergilio called me from the hospital. He was crying. "Pastor, we had to rush Carla to the hospital. The baby was born just now. The baby is dead!"

I was heartbroken. I hung up the telephone and began to cry. I fell to my knees and put my forehead on the floor and began to cry out to God.

"I don't accept it, Jesus."

"I don't accept it. Please, Lord. This lovely child! A child that was prophesied! Born dead! Please, Lord!" I continued to cry out to God. Exactly 17 minutes later, the telephone rang again. It was Vergilio.

"Pastor, the baby came to life. He is alive. They called him Joel. He is a lovely boy."

Now months later, I was in Indonesia and God was reminding me of that dear boy. He spoke to my heart, "Samuel, don't you remember?"

"Yes, Lord, I remember."

"I am the same Lord, Samuel."

"Yes, Lord, I believe."

I began to preach. As I preached, the Holy Ghost came on me and I knew what to do. "Lady," I asked, "Would you come forward?" Everybody was wondering why there was a lady in a men's meeting. "Dr. Daniel told me that this dear woman is pregnant, but the baby in her womb is dead."

She began to tremble. "The Holy Ghost is a miracle working Spirit," I said. I asked her husband to come and stand with her. I anointed both of them with oil. I began to pray. I had no words, but the Spirit began to speak through me: "I am the resurrection and the life. I am the way, the truth and the life. I shall revive this baby. I shall glorify My name."

Some doubted, but when the service was over, some friends took the lady to the hospital, and the doctors confirmed that the baby was alive. Glory to God!

47

Baptism in River Jordan

I have baptized hundreds of people in the Jordan River on my tours of the Holy Lands. I always include a stop at that river so I can baptize new converts. I even baptized one of my grandsons, precious boy, in the Jordan. You can imagine my joy.

One cold November, I baptized 116 Indonesians in the Jordan River. It took one and a half hours to baptize them all. It was so cold. As I waded into the river, I took care not to look back so they wouldn't see the expression on my face. I was afraid if they saw it they would change their minds, but after five minutes, my blood was boiling in the water. The fish kept trying to nibble me, trying to get a little bite from my legs, so I had to keep moving. The people on shore thought I was getting a special blessing, but I was just trying to keep from being eaten by the fish.

I baptized those converts from Indonesia, one by one. Some had been Buddhists; others Muslim. One former Muslim named Mohammed asked me, "Should I change my name?"

"No, sir!" I answered. "It is not your name that gets you into heaven or keeps you out. It is Jesus." I would love to see lots of Mohammeds in heaven, washed in the blood of the Lamb. Hallelujah!

During the baptism I was using a megaphone to speak to the crowd and explain what I was doing. I noticed one man was listening closely. He did not look Indonesian so I knew he was not part of our tour group. When I baptized the last Indonesian, whom do I see standing in the river next to me, but the man who was listening so intently.

He looked like he was in his mid-forties. He said to me with a trembling voice, "I am a Jew from Russia. I've heard every word. I believe everything that you say. Will you baptize me?"

I asked him a few questions, and he answered, "Yes," to every one with a voice full of emotion.

I tell you, heaven was rejoicing. I told the crowd, "Here is a Russian who wants to be baptized!" Everyone cheered. Then I baptized him. The moment I brought him out of the water, I shouted in Russian, "Slava bogo!"

He shouted, "Slava Bogo!" back to me, with a puzzled look on his face.

I could tell that he was wondering, *How does he know Russian?* He did not know that I don't speak Russian, I only know that one phrase. *Slava Bogo* means "Praise God." I learned it while I was in Russia.

Then we hugged each other.

* * *

Something like this had happened to me before. In 1994, I took a group of people from Indonesia and Singapore on a tour of the Holy Land. God moved mightily on that trip. I preached in Jerusalem, and when I gave the altar call, so many people came forward that I cried out, "Lord, help me!" I needed the Lord to give me strength to pray with each one of them. I didn't want anyone to be disappointed. We had a tremendous touch of God in Jerusalem.

A few days later, I baptized 42 people from Indonesia and Singapore in the Jordan River. It was thrilling to baptize so many. When I baptized the last person, I looked up and there was another person standing there. He was in his shirt and trousers, not in white robes like the others. I didn't recognize him.

He looked at me and said, "I've heard you preach. Everything you said, I believe. Please, baptize me."

I said, "Where are you from?"

He said, "I'm from Germany. Please baptize me."

How could I say no? "Your name?" I asked.

"Reiner Deutschland."

What a lovely name. Deutschland means from the land of Germany.

I asked a few questions, then I told all the people who were watching and listening that I was going to baptize one more, this German one.

*   *   *

One of the men in that tour group was a Buddhist from Jakarta. He was a 32-year-old government representative to the television stations named Jimy. Not James, but a Chinese name, Jimy. He had the authority to put text announcements on 12 million television sets all over Indonesia.

He would listen politely to my sermons, but he would not give his heart to the Lord. I could see that the Holy Spirit was working on him. I knew that when the Holy Ghost begins to work on a person, you must leave them alone. Don't mess it up. You need to let the Holy Ghost do the work, because He does a perfect job.

You cannot escape from the Holy Spirit when He deals with you. If you try to run away, He'll go after you. You cannot run away from God. He knows how to speak to you, how to deal with you. If you don't listen, He will speak in a very hard way. If you don't listen to Him in time of health, He will allow sickness to speak to you. If you don't listen to Him when you have healthy, lovely children, suddenly He will speak to you through a very sad way. God knows how to speak to you. Don't run away from Him. Listen to Him. It is so important to obey the voice of the Lord.

I could see that the Spirit of the Lord was speaking to that Buddhist. One day passed. The next day passed. The next day passed. I could tell that his wife was heartbroken because her husband would not give his heart to the Lord. She was weeping and praying that God would save him

On the last Friday of the trip, we went to Masada, then the Dead Sea, Beersheba and then to Tel Aviv. We got to Tel Aviv at 7:30 at night. I was standing in the hotel lobby watching my co-workers give out room keys when Jimy came beside me and said, "Pastor. I want to give my heart to Jesus. Will you baptize me?"

We were leaving on Sunday. I was happy to lead him to the Lord, but I did not see how I could baptize him. I took his hand in mine and led him to the Lord. Then I told him, "If I came to Israel and had this tour just for you, it was worth everything." I was still trying to figure out how to baptize him before we left Israel. I asked, "Do you have a swimming pool in your home in Jakarta?"

"Oh, yes." They had a beautiful swimming pool and a mansion staffed by 20 servants.

"All right," I said. "In December, I am coming to Jakarta. I will baptize you then in your own swimming pool."

Suddenly, I thought, *No, no, no! I don't know what will happen between now and December. Jesus might come. Things in the Middle East are happening so fast. I had better baptize him now. But where?*

Then I remembered that the hotel was right next to the Mediterranean Sea. You could see the beautiful blue water from the rooms. I had never baptized anybody in the Mediterranean Sea. I had baptized many people in the Jordan River and a few in the Dead Sea, but never in the Mediterranean.

"Jimy," I said. "tomorrow morning I will baptize you in the Mediterranean." I told the group, "Six A.M. wake-up call."

At seven A.M., all 54 of us were gathered at the seashore. The Israeli police were everywhere. They have very tight security. I did not have permission to hold a baptismal service. I knew that if I asked the police they would say no. So I was going to do it quickly. Before they could get there, it would be over.

We started singing. One of the men played a guitar. Fifty-four of us were praising God. It was the Jewish *Shabbat*, or "Sabbath." Ninety percent of the Jews in Tel Aviv are ungodly. They don't believe in God or go to the synagogue. All that they think about is money, pleasure, politics, and their country. Tel Aviv today is like Sodom and Gomorrah. On Saturday mornings, one and a half million people, go to the sea—it is their "church". The beach was packed with Jewish families enjoying their day off. As we sang, they gathered around us to see what was going on with those Indonesians.

I realized that I needed to act quickly. I got hold of Jimy's hand. "Let's go." We waded into the marvelous Mediterranean Sea. Waves were hitting us. It was a beautiful day. I waded in up to my waist, then turned to face the crowd on shore.

Everyone was watching. I had three questions. "DO YOU BELIEVE, BUDDHIST, JESUS IS THE SON OF THE LIVING GOD?" I asked.

He said, "Yes, I do."

Jimy's wife had waded into the water with her clothes on so she could get a picture. Tears were rolling down her cheeks. *Jimy's getting baptized.*

I asked Jimy, "DO YOU BELIEVE JESUS DIED ON THE CROSS FOR YOUR SINS?"

"Yes, I do."

Heaven was rejoicing. So was I!

"DO YOU PROMISE TO LIVE FOR JESUS FOR THE REST OF YOUR LIFE?"

"I do."

At that moment, a big wave came and threw us both into the water. God baptized both of us. I was knocked off my feet and lost hold of Jimy. I fell into the water. People came running to help us, but at that point, what could they do?

Jimy turned to me, "You are so strong. How did you hold me?" But I had not held him. The Lord must have held him. The Lord hit him with the wave, just the way the Lord hit Jacob in the side and turned Jacob into Israel.

I still hadn't baptized him. "It is not over yet, Jimy. Let's get back again where we were. I baptize you in the name of the Father, the Son and the Holy Ghost." I put him in the water. He came out, hugging me and crying.

When we waded ashore, a group of Jews gathered around us asking, "What is going on? What is it?"

What an opportunity! What joy! To be able to tell them! We explained how Jesus said, "Go to the whole world and preach the Gospel, baptizing them in the name of the Father, the Son and the Holy Ghost. We are doing exactly what Jesus had said, two thousand years ago," we explained. "This man was a Buddhist, but now he believes in Jesus. I baptized him just now."

One of our party, a Chinese lady from Jakarta, turned to this one who was asking all the questions, and asked, "Do you want to be baptized, too?"

The Jewish man ran away.

Jimy said to me, "When I go back to Indonesia, I am going to advertise every meeting where you will be. Twelve million television sets all over the country will announce your meetings—in Jakarta, Bali, and Surabaya. I want to let the whole country know where you are preaching."

Isn't God wonderful? Our God is a great God.

48

On Patmos

On May 5, 1998, I went to the island of Patmos. Patmos is the island where the Apostle John received revelation from God. He wrote it all down and this book became the Book of Revelation.

Patmos is a small volcanic island in the Aegean Sea. It has been owned by Turkey and Italy and now Greece. A few thousand people live there, mostly fishermen and their families in a few small villages. It takes 11 hours to reach Patmos by boat from Piraeus, a seaport near Athens.

I went to Patmos to be alone, to fast and pray and rest. I rented a small house that sits by itself at the end of a road, near a monastery. I lived there alone. There was a small chapel next to the house called St. Nicola Chapel, where I would go to pour out my heart to God. I often sat on a large flat rock where I prayed, meditated and read the Bible. Several times I went to St. John's cave, the very place where the apostle received the revelation from God.

While I was there, I wondered, *Will God send another angel to me?* I had seen nine angels in my life as I have described in my book, *Heavenly Beings, Angels, Are They Real?* I had seen an angel at the home of my childless friends in Scotland; on the train to Perth; on the fiery plane above Italy; and in the midst of war in Beirut. One time in Asyut, thousands of people in the audience screamed and shouted because they saw angels standing behind me with wings outstretched. I didn't see them, but the congregation did.

In my little house on Patmos, for the first month, there were times when I was alone in the house and felt such a strong presence of the Lord that I asked God if an angel was coming soon. But the answer was no. One night I dreamt about an angel. I dreamt I was standing on a cliff and that an angel was telling me to fly. I let go and flew in the most marvelous way. I landed gently, peacefully, but it was only a dream.

A month and two weeks after I arrived—on June 20, 1998, at 3:50 A.M.—suddenly my room was full of light. There were no lights anywhere near the house. I knew the sun would rise at 6:30 in the morning, but this was not the sunrise.

When I looked, I saw five angels. The two on my right side had no wings. The other three on my left side had wonderful wings. The five angels formed a circle around me. I saw them clearly: their hands, their bright faces, and their hair. They smiled at me. They looked like human beings but full of light. They wore beautiful white robes that reached the floor.

I was trembling, shaking. I wanted to cry, but I couldn't. Then the angel on my right side said, "We are the five angels, from the five continents." I know that geographers divide the world into more than five continents, but this is what the angels said.

Suddenly I was in a vision. In the Spirit I could see that I was in a great meeting, with a great multitude of God's children from many nations. I was standing on the platform, behind the pulpit. I was preaching in English. I had an interpreter on my left side. He had dark hair and wore a gray suit, but I was not sure what language he was interpreting my message into. I was prophesying:

"My church, you preach love, teach love, but you need to practice love, and to show love. There is a need for unity in My body. There are many divisions among you. My Spirit will not move and work where there is no unity. There is carnality in My church. I desire a holy people. I died to make you holy."

I was wide awake, but lost in the spirit. My eyes were open, and as I looked out over the great multitude, the five angels came toward me. I backed up, three, four meters. I was going to fall, but some power kept me from falling.

Then the angels began to give me messages, one after another. The multitude was listening, and I believe they saw the angels, too. I saw that the Lord is going to reveal Himself in many parts of the world through the ministry of angels.

The angels told me, "What you see and hear, tell it to the nations." The angel of China, India, and Australia had a long trumpet. The angel of Israel and the whole Middle East had a sickle in his hand. The angel of Europe had a scale. The angel of Africa had a sword. And the angel of North and South America had a bowl of judgment.

One by one, each angel told me about the disasters that would come to their part of the world. I saw disasters in every part of the world: earthquakes, flooding, fires, strong winds, and famine. Millions would die of natural disasters, nuclear disasters, starvation and thirst. The United Nations would be broken to pieces. The Eiffel Tower would fall, and the world market in New York would collapse. I saw skyscrapers in New York tumble to the ground. This was three years before 9/11. I saw ships sinking. Great floods in many parts of the world.

The angels also showed me that there would be a great spiritual awakening. Bondages would be broken, barriers removed. Millions would turn to Christ. The church would be purified, protected and readied for the final day.

Those who had refused Jesus, refused His message of love, would hate each other, kill one another and be destroyed. I saw blood over many countries. I saw destruction, fire and smoke rising to heaven.

During this time of revelation, I was shaking. I wanted to cry, but the tears would not come. So much disaster. So much destruction.

I cried, "Lord, what about Your children?"

The angel said, "I will prepare them. They will look for My appearing. Many will cry to Me, and I will save them. I shall perform mighty miracles for them and show them My power."

"Lord," I cried. "It is all bad news, all destruction. Is there any good news?"

The Lord said, "The final day has come. Judgment day is here. My love has been refused, now My anger has come."

I was so shaken, I thought, *I can't bear it anymore.*

The whole world was shaken. "In a short time," I heard the angel say, "This is going to happen."

I saw the five angels surround the earth, lifting up their wings and their hands toward heaven, saying, "All glory to the Lord of heaven and earth. Now the time has come. He will glorify His Son. The earth shall be burned and destroyed. All things shall pass away. The new earth shall come." The angels ascended toward heaven, then went off in five different directions. I knew that they had already begun their duties.

After I received the messages from the five angels, I could not move for more than an hour. For a moment, I thought that I was paralyzed. I was lost in the presence of God. I did not know if I should cry or not. I was trembling from head to foot.

I asked the Lord, "Shall I leave Patmos now?"

"No. I have brought you here for a purpose."

"I am in Your hands, Lord. Let Your will be done." Then I continued, "Lord, the messages the angels brought are words of judgment. I have always preached about Your love."

"You are the instrument, the channel," the Lord said. "You are privileged to be chosen to give My message."

I answered, "Your will be done."

For a long time I could not move. I was in the presence of a Holy God. For three days I did not leave the house. I prayed, fasted, and sought the mind of God. I wrote down everything that the Lord brought to my memory.

When I left Patmos, I prayed that God would fill me with His love; that the Holy Spirit would anoint me; and that the Lord would continue to use me for His glory. I wanted my whole life, my being—body, soul, and spirit—to be completely surrendered on the altar; sanctified through and through.

I wanted my heart to be pure and cleansed in the blood of the Lamb. I wanted my mind to be the mind of Christ, and I wanted my body to be the temple of the Holy Ghost.

The King is coming! Maranatha! The Lord is returning! Do everything to be ready and to let others hear about the wonderful love of Jesus!

49

On Television in the Middle East

In 1967, when I was 37 years old, the Lord told me that one day I would preach before millions in the Middle East on television. It happened while I was preaching in our Salem Evangelistic Center in Beirut. I was standing in front of the whole church. I paused to listen and heard, *You will preach to millions in the Middle East on television.* This was back in the days before satellite TV It seemed impossible. Illogical! Inconceivable!

Everybody who heard it said, "It's impossible. Not in the Middle East. Not on television." It was hard to imagine how it could happen. Some criticized, saying, "It is his wishful thinking! He gave that prophecy because that is what he would like to have happen."

I myself thought, *Lord, that was a very strange prophecy, but I believe You!*

A few years later, I thought the day had come to pass because a Lebanese man who owned a TV station videotaped our service in Beirut, but he never aired the tape.

Then in 2005, Benny Hinn called my wife and asked to meet with me. As soon as I got back to Pasadena, I invited him to our home. My whole family was there—my wife, our four boys and their wives, and my daughter and her husband. We all gave him a big welcome.

We sat at my dinner table sharing for four hours straight. Benny Hinn is a very humble man. Not everybody agrees with the way he ministers, but who am I to speak anything against a brother who is preaching Jesus?

While we were sitting at the dinner table, I shared how I had seen a vision of the huge 2004 tsunami six days before it happened. We were grieved over the loss and destruction.

Benny said he wanted to interview me on his television show. Then he said something that warmed my heart. "I have bought a television channel that broadcasts to one hundred million people in the Arab world including Saudi Arabia and all the Arab countries. And I want you to be the first speaker on that television program."

I was amazed. I thought of the prophecy. Nearly 40 years had past. Now I would be preaching to millions in the Middle East on television!

I cannot get into Egypt or Syria, but they cannot stop my voice! In early 2005, I prepared eight messages in Benny Hinn's studio, just a short drive from my home in Pasadena. I brought my Egyptian interpreter and my singer and we recorded six programs in Arabic, with music and preaching. It was tremendous! God had opened the door for me to broadcast into the Arab world from America! The prophecy was fulfilled.

Thousands of my Egyptian friends couldn't believe that they could see me—Doctorian—on their televisions! They all know that I cannot enter Egypt, but there I was on the screen right in front of them. I was also on television in Saudi Arabia, Lebanon and Syria. We got emails and calls from all over the Arab world from excited friends who had seen me on television.

I also appeared on Benny Hinn's show in America. I was humbled when Benny introduced me as "a true prophet of God." I spoke about my visit with the five angels. People from all across America began to order my book about angels. We have sold, so far, over 25,000 copies of my books. We never have had such a response before. The telephone company lines were jammed with people ordering my small book.

* * *

I have spent much of my life preaching in difficult countries. The Middle East is the most difficult area of the world. You don't hear of evangelists going to Syria or Egypt. Some might go as tourists, but not to evangelize. I've preached in Iraq and Jordan. In Lebanon, the Lord has used our ministry to bear much fruit. In Egypt I have led thousands and thousands to the Lord, more than in any other county in the Middle East.

Young people, if we ever needed laborers, it is now. If we ever needed preachers full of the Holy Spirit, who can take the Gospel to the far corners of the earth, it is now. Perhaps God is calling you through my life story. I trust that if He calls, you will obey. I trust that you will become winners of souls for the glory of Jesus.

Our family is settled in Pasadena now, where our Armenian church has grown so large that in 2005 we moved into a new building. Our Armenian congregation uses the founding church for the whole Nazarene denomination—Bresee Church of the Nazarene in Pasadena—for their services! Our son, Paul, is pastor.

We still have a flat in Beirut in our Peniel building, up on the side of the mountain east of Beirut. I go there often to preach and to encourage our workers. We still have a Christian day school in Beirut. We pay the school fees of many children in different schools in Beirut, and all over the world, so they can go to Christian school and we support many orphans financially.

Today we can seat one thousand people in our Salem Center. The church is about 60 percent Arab and 40 percent Armenian. At the Salem Center we preach in Armenian or translate into Armenian if the preacher uses another language. Four Armenian brothers lead the worship. They used to perform in nightclubs, but then they all gave their lives to Jesus, so now they lead our worship. We have also built a second evangelistic center in another part of the city called Bethlehem Center. At the Bethlehem Center we preach in Arabic. Armenians also attend that church, but they all understand Arabic.

We pray that the Lord will bring lasting peace to Lebanon. We pray that He gives us strength to continue the work of the Lord in that needy part of the Bible lands. By the grace of God we shall continue to minister as long as He gives us breath or until the trumpet sounds!

I trust that this life story will be a rich blessing to you. God will not fail you if you depend on Him. If you are not saved, cry out to Him. Acknowledge who He is and who you are. Admit your need for God. Ask Him to save you. He will save you and change you. He will sanctify you and make you whole. He has done both for me.

EPILOGUE

Even though Samuel Doctorian is now 76, he still travels the world preaching the good news of Jesus Christ. He is only at home, in Pasadena, California, for less than two months a year. Even so, despite his busy schedule, the Doctorian family is very close, and Samuel speaks to his family daily by telephone. All of Samuel and Naomi's children are married and three out of five live nearby. Two of their sons, Paul and Danny, and their families, live next door to Samuel and Naomi. Samuel Jr. and his family are five minutes away. Jasmine and her husband live in Baton Rouge, Louisiana where they pastor a church, while Luther and his wife live in Nashville, Tennessee where he runs a recording studio. Samuel and Naomi have 9 grandchildren, including twins born to Luther and Rebecca in late 2005, and a baby girl born to Samuel, Jr. and Arpi in early 2006. All of the children are following the Lord, and three of the four sons work with Bible Land Mission.

Samuel and Naomi have been married for 54 years. Samuel says, "Naomi reads the Bible more than I. She goes to every prayer meeting. She encourages me. She never hinders the work of the Lord, though she often asks, 'Samuel, when will you slow down?'"

Donations in support of Bible Land Mission can be made at www.Biblelandmission.org or mailed to Bible Land Mission, P.O. Box 41299, Pasadena, CA 91114, USA.

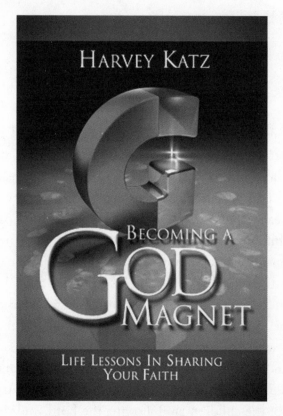

Harvey Katz

BECOMING A GOD MAGNET

Life Lessons In Sharing Your Faith

If you've ever had your heart pound as you opened your mouth to share your faith . . . this book is for you!

Many Christians view evangelism as a chore, a responsibility they dread. Harvey Katz has good news: God wants to attract people to Jesus Christ through your life . . . in a relaxed, natural, joyful way. In this book, Harvey Katz will show you how.

Charlene Curry

THE GENERAL'S LADY
God's Faithfulness to a Military Spouse

Charlene Curry recounts all the joys and challenges of being a career military spouse and how she triumphed over difficulties by relying on a source of spiritual power that transformed her life.

Major General Jerry R. Curry

FROM PRIVATE TO GENERAL
*An African American Soldier
Rises Through the Ranks*

Major General Jerry Curry vividly describes his life journey of military missions, powerful positions, and his relationship with the true source of authority—his Father in heaven.

Fern C. Willner

WHEN FAITH IS ENOUGH
*A Safari of Destiny that Reveals
Principles to Live By*

A faith-inspiring story of a missionary wife and mother of seven relying completely on God in the heart of Africa. Accompanying workbook also available for discussion groups in 2007